CONTEMPORARY & TRADITIONAL
RESOURCES FOR WORSHIP LEADERS

The

ABINGDON
WORSHIP
ANNUAL
2013

EDITED BY MARY J. SCIFRES & B. J. BEU

Abingdon Press
Nashville

THE ABINGDON WORSHIP ANNUAL 2013
CONTEMPORARY AND TRADITIONAL RESOURCES FOR WORSHIP LEADERS

Copyright © 2012 by Abingdon Press

This book is printed on acid-free paper.

Library of Congress Cataloging-in-Publication Data

ISBN 978-1-4267-4679-6
ISSN 1545-9322

All scripture quotations unless noted otherwise are taken from the New Revised Standard Version of the Bible, copyright 1989 by the Division of Christian Education of the National Council of the Churches of Christ in the United States of America. Used by permission. All rights reserved.

Scripture quotations from THE MESSAGE. Copyright © by Eugene H. Peterson 1993, 1994, 1995, 1996, 2000, 2001, 2002. Used by permission of NavPress Publishing Group.

Liturgies marked UMH are based on *The United Methodist Hymnal*, copyright 1989 by The United Methodist Publishing House. Used by permission.

12 13 14 15 16 17 18 19 20 21—10 9 8 7 6 5 4 3 2 1

MANUFACTURED IN THE UNITED STATES OF AMERICA

CONTENTS

May

June

July

August

September

October

November

December

CONTRIBUTORS

INDEXES

ONLINE CONTENTS

The following materials are found only in the Abingdon Worship Annual 2013 *section at www.abingdonpress.com/ downloads. Instructions on how to view these materials in your browser, or download them to your computer, are available at the site. PLEASE NOTE: This file is password protected; please see page viii below for the password.*

CONTENTS

INTRODUCTION

To worship God is an awesome experience. To lead others in the worship of God is a unique calling and a humbling opportunity. Into this opportunity, we offer *The Abingdon Worship Annual 2013* as a resource and partner in your planning process. The task of planning worship can be filled with joy and excitement; it can also be plagued with the worries of deadlines and multiple responsibilities. In order to ease some of those worries, this resource offers words for worship for each Sunday of the lectionary year, along with suggestions for many of the "high" holy days. For each worship service, suggestions are provided in an orderly fashion to also provide a flow for your worship service. Feel free, however, to re-order or pick and choose the various resources to fit the needs of your worship services and congregations.

In *The Abingdon Worship Annual 2013*, each week's entry provides a specific thematic focus arising from one or more of the week's scriptures. That theme, along with corresponding scripture imagery, is then carried out through each of the suggested prayers and litanies. For those who are working with contemporary worship services, alternative ideas for those settings are offered for each service as well. Each entry includes a Call to Worship, Opening Prayer, Prayers of Confession and Assurance of Pardon, Offertory, and Benedictions. Many entries include Communion Resources. Starting this year, those who purchase the *Abingdon Worship Annual 2013* will be able to access the full text of the resource, along with additional materials, online. Please visit the AWA 2013 section of www.abingdonpress.com/

downloads, click on the link to the AWA 2013, and when prompted enter the following password: **worship2013.** At the site, you will find all of these resources available electronically for worship printing preparation. You will also find hymn suggestions for each entry hyperlinked to that day's entry. We have ordered each day's suggestions to fit the Basic Pattern of Christian Worship, reflecting a flow that leads from a time of gathering and praise, into a time of receiving and responding to the Word, and ending with a time of sending forth. The Praise Sentences and Contemporary Gathering Words fit the spontaneous and informal nature of many non-traditional worship styles and easily fit into the time for gathering and praise. Use this resource as flexibly as you need, turning to the scripture index of this and previous volumes when different themes or scriptures are required.

In response to requests from many of our readers, we are again offering a number of Communion liturgies on the web site. These are compiled from more than ten years of resources prepared by our many talented writers. Many of the Communion resources follow the pattern of the Great Thanksgiving; others are prayers of preparation and consecration for the celebration of the Eucharist. You will also find various prayers, litanies, and responsive readings that are particularly related to Communion themes and Eucharistic imagery. Scripture and seasonal references are provided for each suggestion, but you will want to use them interchangeably throughout the corresponding seasons. For instance, the Communion service for Transfiguration Sunday could be used at any time during the season of Epiphany.

The Abingdon Worship Annual complements several other resources from Abingdon Press. As you plan lectionary-based worship, preachers will find *The Abingdon Preaching Annual* an invaluable help. Worship planners and preachers can also rely upon *Prepare! An Ecumenical Music and Worship Planner* or *The United Methodist Music and Worship Planner* for excellent music suggestions of hymns, praise songs, vocal solos, and choral anthems. Together, these three resources provide the words, the music, and the preaching guidance to plan integrated and coordinated worship services.

As you begin your worship planning, we encourage you to spend time with the scriptures for the day, reflecting upon them thoughtfully and prayerfully. Review the thematic ideas suggested in this resource and then read through the many words for worship provided that speak to the theme. Listen for the words that speak to you. Let this resource be the starting point for your worship planning, letting the Spirit guide you and allowing God's Word to flow through you. Worship that arises from careful and caring plans honors the God who gave such careful planning to our creation and gives such caring attention to our world and our needs.

All contributions in *The Abingdon Worship Annual* are based upon readings from the Revised Common Lectionary. However, the contributing authors represent a wide variety of denominational and theological backgrounds, so the words before you will vary in style and content. Feel free to combine or adjust the words within these pages to fit the needs of your congregation and the style of your worship services. Some authors use very inclusive language; others refer to more traditional words. Be creative, even with the words given to you. *Kingdom* can become "realm" or "kin-dom." *Lord* can become "God" or "Christ" or "Most Holy One." As you use these words, integrate your own theology of worship and liturgy so that the words speak to you and your congregation most meaningfully. You'll find the reprint permission for worship given on the copyright page of this book, and we do request that you do give credit to both the author and the resource. Trust God's guidance, and enjoy a wonderful year of worship and praise with your congregations! We wish you God's blessings as you seek to share Christ's word and offer experiences of the Holy Spirit in your work and worship!

Mary J. Scifres and B. J. Beu, Editors

JANUARY 1, 2013

Watch Night / New Year

Mary J. Scifres

COLOR
White

SCRIPTURE READINGS
Ecclesiastes 3:1-13; Psalm 8; Revelation 21:1-6a; Matthew 25:31-46

THEME IDEAS
Time is never more evident than at the turning of the year. Today's scriptures reflect this focus on time: time for every matter under heaven, time to proclaim God's majesty, time to imagine a new heaven and new earth, time to face God's judgment for our actions or inactions. As you prepare this worship service, let time become a way of focusing people's confession of the past year, even as it offers hope for the new year. In confession, we shed past regrets and sorrows, creating space for grace and hope.

INVITATION AND GATHERING

Call to Worship *(Ecclesiastes 3, John 4, John 5, New Year)*
(This call leads smoothly into Brian Wren's hymn "This Is a Day of New Beginnings." See additional hymn suggestions on the CD-ROM supplemental materials.)

The time has come and now is.
A new year is being born!
The time has come and now is.
A new beginning is ours in Christ!
The time has come and now is.
**A new opportunity is dawning for grace and joy
as we leave past sorrows behind.**

Opening Prayer (Psalm 8, Revelation 21)

Ancient God, ever renewing your creation,
draw us into newness of life,
through Christ Jesus and your Holy Spirit.
Even as you lay a foundation for our lives
that is deeper than the oceans
and mightier than the mountains of this earth,
instill within us and throughout our world
the hope of a new heaven and a new earth.
Plant your grace and hope within us,
that we may experience growth in your realm
every day of our lives,
in the name of Jesus the Christ,
who overcame death
to bring us life anew. Amen.

PROCLAMATION AND RESPONSE

Call to Confession (Ecclesiastes 3)

To everything there is a season: a time to weep, to mourn,
to tear, to throw away. Let us embrace this time of confession together.

Prayer of Confession (Ecclesiastes 3, Revelation 21, New Year)

Ancient and Future God,
forgive us when we sink so deeply in our past,
that we miss moments of grace in the present.
Help us shed the regrets and sorrows of this past year,
even as we build on the joys and growth
we have discovered along the way.

Guide our steps,
   that we might move forward
      as children of faith and hope.
In Christ's name, we pray. Amen.

—OR—

Prayer of Confession (Matthew 25)
God of sheep and goats,
   forgive us when act like goats—
      neglecting the needs of your world,
      forgetting to show compassion and kindness,
      withholding love and grace to those in need.
Call us to lives of righteousness,
   that we may walk as the sheep of your pasture—
      journeying with those who are in greatest need,
      caring for those who are most alone,
      and loving those who are most forgotten.

Words of Assurance (Ecclesiastes 3)
To everything there is a season.
As forgiven children of God,
   we are invited to enter a season of healing
   and leave the time of brokenness behind.

Passing the Peace of Christ (Ecclesiastes 3)
With the joy of grace and forgiveness, let us move forward into times of laughter, dancing, building and gathering. Let us share this joy and laughter, as we pass the peace of Christ to one another.

Introduction to the Word (Ecclesiastes 3)
In this time before us, let us keep silence.
(A time of silence may follow here and after each scripture reading.)
Listen, not only with your ears, but with your hearts and minds as well.

Response to the Word (Ecclesiastes 3, Revelation 21, Matthew 25)
There is a season for every matter under heaven.
   But in every season,

3

> God calls us to be a people
> of justice and mercy.
There is a time for each and every thing.
> **But at all times,**
> **Christ reminds us to be a people**
> **of prayer and connection.**
There is a time for remembering the past
and a time for living into the future.
> **But today and always,**
> **the Spirit lives and moves within us,**
> **that we may be a people of new beginnings.**

THANKSGIVING AND COMMUNION

Invitation to the Offering (Matthew 25)
Christ calls to us in the voice of the hungry and through the cries of the needy. Let us answer Christ's call as we share our gifts and offerings with the church and its ministries to meet the needs of God's world.

Offering Prayer (Revelation 21, Matthew 25)
Eternal God,
> bless these gifts,
> > that they may be seeds of new beginnings
> > > for those touched by the ministries
> > > > of your church.
Let the promise of joy in the midst of sorrow,
> the promise of hope in the midst of despair,
> > shine through these gifts
> > > and the gifts of our lives
> > > > as we seek to serve you. Amen.

Great Thanksgiving
It is right, and a good and joyful thing,
> always and everywhere to give thanks to you,
> Almighty God, creator of heaven and earth.

From ancient times,
> to the promise of a new heaven and earth,

you have revealed your presence to us.
In the time of creation,
    you formed us in your image
    and brought forth the earth in all of its abundance.
When we fell short, you stood firm and loved us
    with steadfastness and hope.
During times of sinfulness and disobedience,
    you delivered us into a time of grace
    and forgiveness.
In times of rebellion and confusion,
    you spoke to us in the voices of the prophets.

And so, with your people on earth,
    and all the company of heaven,
    we praise your name
    and join their unending hymn, saying:
    Holy, holy, holy Lord, God of power and might,
        heaven and earth are full of your glory.
    Hosanna in the highest. Blessed is the one
        who comes in the name of the Lord.
    Hosanna in the highest.

Holy are you and blessed is your holy name.
In the fullness of time, you sent your Son, Jesus Christ,
    to reveal your powerful love in the world.
In this time of new beginnings,
    Christ proclaims to us life in the face of death
    and hope in the midst of despair.
Through Christ's powerful love and endless grace,
    we are invited into your new heaven and earth,
    even in this time and place.
In this time of remembering the past
    and looking to the future,
    we remember Jesus' time
    of endings and beginnings.

On the night before his death, Jesus took bread,
    gave thanks to you, broke the bread,

gave it to the disciples, saying:
"Take, eat; this is my body which is given for you.
Do this in remembrance of me."
When the supper was over, Jesus took the cup,
offered thanks and gave it to the disciples, saying:
"Drink from this, all of you;
this is my life in the new covenant, poured out
for you and for many, for the forgiveness of sins.
Do this, as often as you drink it,
in remembrance of me."

And so, in remembrance of these
your mighty acts of love and grace,
and with the hope of new beginnings
and new life in Christ Jesus,
we offer ourselves in praise and thanksgiving
in union with Christ's love for us,
as we proclaim the mystery of faith.
Christ has died.
Christ is risen.
Christ will come again.

Communion Prayer
Pour out your Holy Spirit
on all of us gathered here
and on these gifts of bread and wine,
that this may be a time for releasing past regrets,
leaning on past wisdom,
and moving into God's new future.
May these gifts of memory and substance
be for us new life in Christ,
nourished by the love of God.
May we be for the world the body of Christ,
a people of new beginnings and new hope,
redeemed and renewed
by Christ's love and grace.
By your Spirit,
make us one with Christ,
one with each other,
and one in ministry to all the world;

make us new creations in your holy image
until Christ comes in final victory,
    when we will feast at your heavenly banquet
      for all of eternity.
Through Jesus Christ,
    with the Holy Spirit in your holy Church,
      all honor and glory is yours, Almighty God,
      now and forever more. Amen.

Giving the Bread and Cup
(The bread and wine are given to the people, with these or other words of blessing.)
New life in Christ, given to you.
The love of Christ, flowing through you.

SENDING FORTH

Benediction (Revelation 21, 1 Corinthians 13)
May the God of eternity strengthen you with love.
May the Christ of new life inspire you with hope.
May the Spirit of new beginnings empower you
    with faith.

CONTEMPORARY OPTIONS

Contemporary Gathering Words (Ecclesiastes 3)
This is God's time, a time to let the past die
    as Christ births our new future.
This is God's time, a time to weed out regrets
    as the Spirit plants hope for the future.
This is God's time, a time to forsake patterns of death
    as the Holy One gives us the promise of new life.
This is God's time, a time to worship the One
    of endings and new beginnings.

Praise Sentences (Psalm 8)
Praise God for the majesty of the earth!
Praise God for the beauty of the heavens!

Praise God for the majesty of the earth!
Praise God for the beauty of the heavens!

Praise Sentences (Psalm 8)

Look at the heavens and sing God's praise!
Look at the heavens and sing God's praise!
Imagine God's new heaven and earth...
hope that is ours in Christ Jesus!
New heaven and earth...
hope that is ours in Christ Jesus!

JANUARY 6, 2013

Epiphany of the Lord
Deborah Sokolove

COLOR

White

SCRIPTURE READINGS

Isaiah 60:1-6; Psalm 72:1-7, 10-14; Ephesians 3:1-12; Matthew 2:1-12

THEME IDEAS

The people of God are to be a light to the world, a beacon leading everyone toward peace and justice. Like the magi who followed the star to Bethlehem, all who follow the light of God will rejoice in the presence of the Holy One.

INVITATION AND GATHERING

Call to Worship (Isaiah 60)
Arise, shine, for your light has come!
The glory of the Holy One has risen upon you!
**Our spirits soar at the dawning of the light
that illumines our darkness.
Our hearts rejoice at God's abundant grace.**
Lift up your eyes and look around,
for God has pity on the weak,
and redeems the oppressed from violence.

9

Come to Bethlehem with the magi,
following the star of God's glory,
and proclaiming the good news of Jesus,
who is the Christ.
Arise, shine, for your light has come!
The glory of the Holy One has risen upon you!
We shall see with eyes made new.
We shall see and be radiant!

Opening Prayer (Isaiah 60, Psalm 72)

Holy Light of all the nations,
shine upon us and upon all humankind.
Fill us with your Spirit,
that we may be beacons of hope to all the earth,
bringing the peace of Christ
to everyone we meet. Amen.

PROCLAMATION AND RESPONSE

Prayer of Confession (Psalm 72, Ephesians 3)

Holy Source of righteousness and peace,
we have failed to share the good news
of your love and grace.
We have not been generous with one another,
finding fault instead of extending compassion.
We have not judged one another with righteousness,
assigning blame instead of seeking understanding.
We have not defended the cause of the poor,
hoarding our wealth instead of sharing it
with those in need.
Forgive our selfish ways,
and help us live in the light
of your righteousness and justice.

Words of Assurance (Isaiah 60, Psalm 72)

The Holy One reaches out to us in compassion,
delivering us when we call,
and filling us with radiant love.
In the light of Christ, you are forgiven.
In the light of Christ, you are forgiven.

Glory to God.
Amen.

Passing the Peace of Christ
In the mystery of grace, share signs of God's peace:
May the peace of Christ be with you, always.
May the peace of Christ be with you, always.

Introduction to the Word or Prayer of Preparation (Isaiah 60, Matthew 2)
Light of the world, wisdom of God,
    maker of all things,
    as you led the Magi to Bethlehem,
    lead us to hear and understand your holy word.
    Fill our hearts and minds with your holy light,
    that we may be radiant beacons
    of faith and grace. Amen.

Response to the Word (Matthew 2)
Wisdom of God, light of the world, maker of all things,
    we give you thanks for the star
        that led the magi across the desert;
    we give you praise for warning them
        not to return to Herod,
            but to journey home by another road.
May we see and heed the signs
    you place in our lives—
        signs that lead us on the path of peace.
Amen.

THANKSGIVING AND COMMUNION

Offering Prayer (Isaiah 60, Matthew 2)
Maker of all things, wisdom of God, light of the world,
    you fill our hands with abundance
        and our hearts with hope.
As the magi brought their treasure to the infant Jesus,
    we bring these gifts to you with joy,
        that you may use them
            to bring light and peace to our world.
Amen.

Invitation to Communion

Christ be with you.
And also with you.
Lift up your hearts.
We lift them up to God
Let us give our thanks to the Holy One.
It is right to give our thanks and praise.

It is a right, good, and a joyful thing
always and everywhere to give you our thanks,
for filling our hearts with joy
and bathing our lives with your radiant glory.
We praise you for showing the magi
the way to Bethlehem,
for keeping them safe from the rage of Herod,
and for sending them home by a different way.
And so, with your creatures on earth
and all the heavenly chorus,
we praise your name
and join their unending hymn, saying:
Holy, holy, holy One, God of power and might,
heaven and earth are full of your glory.
Hosanna in the highest. Blessed is the one
who comes in your holy name.
Hosanna in the highest.

Holy are you, and holy is your child, Jesus Christ,
who came into the world as a light to the nations,
and who leads us along the paths of righteousness
and peace.
On the night before his death, Jesus took bread,
gave thanks to you, broke the bread,
gave it to the disciples, saying:
"Take, eat; this is my body which is given for you.
Do this in remembrance of me."
When the supper was over, Jesus took the cup,
offered thanks and gave it to the disciples, saying:
"Drink from this, all of you;
this is my life in the new covenant, poured out

for you and for many, for the forgiveness of sins.
Do this, as often as you drink it,
in remembrance of me."
And so, in remembrance of your mighty acts
in Jesus Christ, we proclaim the mystery of faith.
Christ has died.
Christ is risen.
Christ will come again.

Pour out your Holy Spirit on us gathered here,
and on these gifts of bread and wine.
Make them be for us the body and blood of Christ,
that we may be the body of Christ
for the healing of the world.
Light of the world, wisdom of God,
maker of all things, we praise your holy name.
Amen.

SENDING FORTH

Benediction (Isaiah 60)
Arise, shine, for your light has come.
The glory of the Holy One has risen upon you.
May God fill you with light,
and make you shine like a beacon of hope
for everyone to see.

CONTEMPORARY OPTIONS

Contemporary Gathering Words (Isaiah 60)
Arise, shine, for your light has come,
The glory of the Holy One has risen upon you!

Praise Sentences (Psalm 72)
May all fall down before you, Holy One.
May all nations give you honor and glory,
for you deliver the needy when they call;
you rescue the poor and those who have no helper.
May all fall down before you, O God.
May all nations give you honor and glory.

JANUARY 13, 2013

Baptism of the Lord

Joanne Carlson Brown

COLOR
White

SCRIPTURE READINGS
Isaiah 43:1-7; Psalm 29; Acts 8:14-17; Luke 3:15-17, 21-22

THEME IDEAS
In baptism, we are named and claimed as beloved sons and daughters of God. Filled with the Spirit, our lives are never the same again. In today's readings, God's love for God's beloved Son and for all God's beloved daughters and sons shines through. In baptism, God has called each of us by name, claimed each of us as God's own, and given each of us honor and glory. With such radical love washing over us and through us, we are transformed and strengthened to go out and transform the world.

INVITATION AND GATHERING

Call to Worship (Isaiah 43, Luke 3)
A voice comes from heaven and calls us beloved.
Water washes over us and we are changed.
A voice tells us we are precious in God's sight.
Our love, praise, and gratitude
greet the Spirit who blesses us in baptism.

Let us worship the One who calls from the water—
the God of love and transformation.

Opening Prayer (Isaiah 43, Psalm 29, Luke 3)
God of love,
  in this time of worship,
    help us hear you claim us as your own
      as you call us beloved;
    help us claim our own identity
      as precious and honored,
      even in the face of voices
        that tell us differently.
As we reaffirm our baptism this day,
  remind us who we are and whose we are.
Strengthen us to do your work in this world,
  transforming our fragmented communities
    into your Beloved Community—
      which Jesus preached and lived. Amen.

PROCLAMATION AND RESPONSE

Prayer of Confession (Isaiah 43, Psalm 29, Luke 3)
God of water and spirit,
  it is hard to hear your voice calling us beloved
    amid the cacophony of voices around us
      that tell us we are worthless.
Even when we hear your voice,
  it is hard to believe the depth of your love for us
    amid the messages of the world
      that tell us we are far from precious.
Open our ears, Beloved One,
  to hear your voice.
Open our eyes
  to see your amazing presence in this world.
Help us feel your strength
  filling us and enabling us
    to be and do
      what you call us to be and do.

Forgive our doubts, our excuses,
  our inability to hear and see and feel you
    in our lives and in the world around us.
We would claim our true identity:
  the beloved daughters and sons of God—
    washed, named, claimed, and transformed. Amen.

Words of Assurance (Isaiah 43, Psalm 29)
Trust the promise of the One who gave you birth:
  "Do not fear, for I have redeemed you.
  I have called you by name, and you are mine."
There is nothing you can do that will ever change that.
Believe this in your heart and soul and be at peace.

Passing the Peace of Christ (Isaiah 43, Luke 3)
Sisters and brothers, honor one another as God honors
you. Greet one another with the words of grace and peace:
"You are beloved of God."

Prayer of Preparation (Isaiah 43, Psalm 29, Luke 3)
Beloved One,
    open our ears and our hearts to your words—
      words of love, of belonging, of transformation,
        of strength.
Help us claim your words as our own.

Response to the Word (Isaiah 43, Psalm 29, Luke 3)
For these words of love;
  for these promises of identity;
  for the strength these words give us,
    we give you thanks and praise.

THANKSGIVING AND COMMUNION

Invitation to the Offering (Isaiah 43, Luke 3)
We are named and claimed as God's beloved. Our morning offering will enable this church to share this message with all the people in our community who desperately need to hear it. Help us share this good news with the world by giving generously.

Offering Prayer (Isaiah 43)
All-loving and gracious God,
  you have called us by name
    and love us with a fierce tenderness.
In gratitude and praise,
  we offer our love in return—
    love for you and for your people.
May our gifts strengthen your work in the world
  by creating the Beloved Community,
    right here, right now. Amen.

SENDING FORTH

Benediction (Isaiah 43, Psalm 29, Acts 8, Luke 3)
Beloved children of God, go forth as a holy people:
  people who are named and claimed
    by our ever loving God;
  people who claim kinship with Jesus;
  people who possess the strength and purpose
    to carry out God's will
      through the Spirit who enlivens us
      and accompanies us on our journey. Amen.

CONTEMPORARY OPTIONS

Contemporary Gathering Words (Isaiah 43, Luke 3)
Have you heard?
  Heard what?
God has called us by name!
  Why?
To help us know how much God loves us,
how much God wants us to live into our identity
as beloved daughters and sons.
  Wow! That's amazing!
Amazing, indeed.
Let's give praise and thanks
to our awesome, loving God.
Let's worship in Spirit and in love.

Praise Sentences (Psalm 29)
Praise God's glory and strength.
Worship God in holy splendor.
Praise God's glory and strength.
Worship God in holy splendor.
Giving strength to God's people,
God blesses the people with peace.
Giving strength to God's people,
God blesses the people with peace.

JANUARY 20, 2013

Second Sunday after the Epiphany

B. J. Beu

COLOR

Green

SCRIPTURE READINGS

Isaiah 62:1-5; Psalm 36:5-10; 1 Corinthians 12:1-11; John 2:1-11

THEME IDEAS

God delights in God's people and in all of creation. Redemption and reconciliation are not for Israel alone, but extend to the animals and the very land itself. The steadfast love of God we witness in the Psalms is seen in the bestowal of God's spiritual gifts. Since all gifts come from the same Spirit, we are to treasure one another's gifts. Jesus himself exhibits God's delight and the gift of hospitality as he gladdens the wedding of Cana by turning water into wine. God delights in Israel as a groom delights in his bride. Should we be surprised that Jesus' first miracle occurred at a wedding?

INVITATION AND GATHERING

Call to Worship (Psalm 36)

God's steadfast love extends to the heavens.
God's faithfulness reaches to the clouds.

God's righteousness is as strong as the mountains.
God's judgments are as deep as the sea.
God saves humans and animals alike.
The shadow of God's wings protects the land.
Drink from the river of God's delights.
Bathe in the fountain of life.
In God's light we see light.
God's steadfast love saves the upright of heart!

—*OR*—

Call to Worship (1 Corinthians 12)
There are many gifts, but one Spirit.
There are many services, but one Lord.
We offer our gifts in the service of the living Christ.
**We offer our gifts to the service of others
and to the delight of the living God.**

Opening Prayer (Isaiah 62, Psalm 36)
Spirit of God,
your name is revered from mountaintop to the sea;
your glory is praised in the east and in the west,
in the north and in the south;
your Spirit unites us through your wondrous gifts.
Delight in us once more, Holy One,
that the joy of your salvation
may spill over into our lives
and make us one with you
and with one another.
Guide our hearts and minds
into the fullness of your grace,
that we may truly be your people. Amen.

PROCLAMATION AND RESPONSE

Prayer of Confession (1 Corinthians 12)
Gracious God,
the gifts of your Spirit
give us everything we need
to build up your kingdom.

We have not always recognized
   or valued your gifts.
We have acted as if they were ours to use
   for our own purposes.
Forgive our failure of vision
   and our hardness of heart.
May the one who turned water into wine,
   turn our hearts of stone
      into hearts of love and appreciation. Amen.

Words of Assurance (Isaiah 62, Psalm 36)
Drink freely from the river of Christ's grace,
   for you are God's delight.
Splash in the fountain of life,
   for you are God's treasure.
Bathe in waters of God's steadfast love,
   for you are God's own child.
Rejoice in the waters of God's forgiveness!

Response to the Word or Prayer of Thanksgiving (Isaiah 62, Psalm 36, 1 Corinthians 12)
Steadfast God,
   we delight in the river of your love
   and in the fountain of your grace.
May your word of life speak to our hearts,
   that your message of love may abide in us
   as your Spirit abides in your house.
Strengthen us with your generous gifts
   and shine through our lives,
      that we may glorify you
         each and every day.

THANKSGIVING AND COMMUNION

Invitation to the Offering (Isaiah 62, Psalm 36)
As we bathe in the waters of God's love; as we give thanks for the many spiritual gifts we have received, may we be moved with gratitude to share our abundant blessings with the world. In these offerings, may others come to know God's great delight and love for us all!

Offering Prayer (1 Corinthians 12, John 2)
 Divine Spirit,
  as you changed water into wine
   at the wedding at Cana,
    change our simple gifts
     into great joy for those in need.
 Bless and embolden our hearts,
  that we may share our gifts with others,
   that they may discover in themselves
    the gifts of your Spirit. Amen.

SENDING FORTH

Benediction or Call to Worship (Isaiah 62, Psalm 36)
 God's love shines on us like the dawn.
  We are God's delight!
 God's salvation burns in our hearts like a torch.
  We are God's delight!
 God rejoices over us,
 as a bridegroom rejoices over his bride.
  We are God's delight!

CONTEMPORARY OPTIONS

Contemporary Gathering Words (Isaiah 62, Psalm 36)
 God's light shines like the dawn,
 bathing us in love.
  Christ's salvation beckons like a torch,
  kindling the soul to acts of love.
 The Spirit's glory blazes within the soul,
 crowning us with glory.
  In God's light, we see light.

Praise Sentences (Isaiah 62)
 Rejoice and be glad.
 Drink of the river of God's delight!
  Rejoice and be glad!
  Drink of the river of God's delight!

JANUARY 27, 2013

Third Sunday after the Epiphany

Mary J. Scifres

COLOR

Green

SCRIPTURE READINGS

Nehemiah 8:1-3, 5-6, 8-10; Psalm 19; 1 Corinthians 12:12-31a; Luke 4:14-21

THEME IDEAS

First Corinthians 12 reminds us that God's Spirit is ever-present, guiding us toward unity and ministry, supporting and strengthening us for the journey. Equally important is the discussion of various gifts for ministry and service. As the people of God, we are not hearers only, but doers also. In Nehemiah, the Israelites wept when they heard the law of Moses read to them, for they recognized the many ways that they were not living God's law. Yet, Nehemiah invited them to rejoice, for in the hearing, one discovers the possibility for new living. In recognizing the variety of gifts, the early church discovered ways to transform the world and share Christ's love, but always as a community. God's Spirit gives each church, each body of Christ, each community of faith enough resources to live God's word and fulfill Christ's promises. God's Spirit is ever-present, nurturing and empowering us for ministry, even as the Spirit binds us together in unity—for we are far stronger as a community than we are as individuals.

INVITATION AND GATHERING

Call to Worship or Benediction (Psalm 19, 1 Corinthians 12, Luke 4)

The Spirit is calling.
> **We will listen and learn.**

The heavens are shining.
> **We will sing and rejoice.**

The Spirit is moving.
> **We will live the promises of God.**

Opening Prayer or Response to the Word (1 Corinthians 12, Luke 4)

Spirit of God,
> blow through our lives and through our worship.

Bind us together in unity and love,
> that we might be one body in Christ,
> > one body in ministry to the world.

Strengthen us with your power,
> that we might fulfill your call
> > in our lives—
> > > a call to love and service.

Anoint us with your mysterious presence,
> and send us forth
> > to be the hands and feet of Christ.

PROCLAMATION AND RESPONSE

Prayer of Confession (Nehemiah 8, Psalm 19, 1 Corinthians 12)

Spirit of forgiveness and grace,
> you know when we have failed to hear your word
> > or live your love.

Forgive us.
Open our ears to hear
> and our hearts to love.

Spirit of mercy and kindness,
   you know when we have harmed the community
      with our strife and our disagreements.
Forgive us.
Guide us into unity and selflessness,
   that our church might be a true body of Christ,
   that we might be faithful disciples of your Son.
Spirit of truth and righteousness,
   speak to us always,
   move through our lives and through our church,
      that our lives and our ministry
         might tell of your glory
           and display your handiwork.
In trust and gratitude, we pray. Amen.

Words of Assurance (Nehemiah 8, Psalm 19, Luke 4)
The heavens are telling the glory of God.
Do not be sad,
   for the joy of God is our strength and our salvation.
Christ came to proclaim release from captivity,
   even captivity to sin.
In Christ, we are forgiven and made new.
Rejoice, give thanks, and sing!

Passing the Peace of Christ (1 Corinthians 12)
As forgiven and reconciled children of God, let us share
signs of unity with one another in the passing of Christ's
peace.

Introduction to the Word (Nehemiah 8, Psalm 19)
As the ancient Israelites gathered to hear the word of God
for their lives, so now we come to hear God's word for our
lives. May God bless this time of speaking and listening,
that the words spoken and the message received may be
pleasing and acceptable as glorious reflections of Christ's
love.

Response to the Word (Psalm 19)
The law of the Lord is perfect,
enlivening and restoring the soul.

**The words of God are sure and true,
giving wisdom and joy to our lives.**
The promises of Christ endure,
reaching down through all the ages.
**These teachings reflect our hope
and the deepest desires of our hearts.**
They are sweeter than honey,
more precious than gold.
**May the words we have heard
take root in our lives,
that we may be doers of the word.**

THANKSGIVING AND COMMUNION

Invitation to the Offering (Psalm 19)

More precious than all of the world's wealth is the love of
God, given to us in Christ Jesus. May we share this most
precious of gifts in ministry and service, through the sharing of our worldly wealth. Will the ushers now wait upon
us to receive today's offering.

Offering Prayer (1 Corinthians 12)

Spirit of generosity and love,
flow through these gifts and offerings.
Work in the ministries of our church,
that Christ's love may be seen clearly
and felt completely
in all that we say
and in all that we do.
In Christ's name, we pray. Amen.

SENDING FORTH

Benediction (1 Corinthians 12)

You are the body of Christ,
individual members of a community of love and faith.
**We go forth as Christ's hands and feet,
Christ's heart and mind,
to share Christ's love and ministry of grace.**
Go forth in unity and joy.

CONTEMPORARY OPTIONS

Contemporary Gathering Words (Psalm 19, 1 Corinthians 12)
Come into God's presence,
listening for a word of love.
Come, Holy Spirit, come.
Gather with friends, new and old,
to sing praises and glory to God.
Come, Holy Spirit, come.
Come, Holy Spirit, gather us in.
Unify our worship and ministry.
Strengthen our understanding of your word,
that we might live and serve in unity and love.
Come, Holy Spirit, come.

Praise Sentences (Psalm 19)
Earth and heaven rejoice in beauty and glory.
Sing of God's amazing gifts!
The sun and the stars give light to all.
Sing of God's amazing gifts!
God's word shows us the way of life.
Sing of God's amazing gifts!

FEBRUARY 3, 2013

Fourth Sunday after the Epiphany
Mary Petrina Boyd

COLOR

Green

SCRIPTURE READINGS

Jeremiah 1:4-10; Psalm 71:1-6; 1 Corinthians 13:1-13; Luke 4:21-30

THEME IDEAS

God calls and sends us to do the work of loving and redeeming the world. When the call came to Jeremiah, he objected that he was too young. When Jesus brought God's call to his own community, they resisted hearing the word from someone they knew. Human beings resist the call of God. We fail to trust the in-breaking of God's new life. We cannot seem to accept God's message of love and possibility. Yet, God knows us and knows our potential far better than we ever will.

INVITATION AND GATHERING

X**Call to Worship (Psalm 71)**

God is our refuge,
our rock and our shelter.
The Lord is our hope,
who rescues us from trouble.

God knows us from birth,
nurturing us with love and care.
Praise be to our God!
Praise God at all times!

X *Opening Prayer (Jeremiah 1, 1 Corinthians 13)*
You know us, O God;
you understand our worries and fears.
Open our hearts to your transforming love,
that your word may grow within us—
building a community that bears all things,
believes all things, and hopes all things. Amen.

PROCLAMATION AND RESPONSE

Prayer of Confession (Jeremiah 1, 1 Corinthians 13)
God of love,
when you call us to serve, we are full of excuses:
we are too young or too old,
we don't know enough,
we don't have the skills that you need.
We would rather not speak your words of truth.
We would much rather stay where we are,
than trust you to lead us on adventures
of growth and love.
We are arrogant, insisting on our own way,
sure that our plan is better than yours.
We are envious, boastful, rude, irritable, and resentful.
Give us the wisdom and courage to follow your call,
even when it leads to places
we cannot clearly see.
Teach us to trust your love
as we answer your summons,
that through our response,
others may be blessed. Amen.

Words of Assurance (Psalm 71, 1 Corinthians 13)
O God, you are our hope,
our place of safety in a world of change.

You put your word within us,
    that we may have the words we need
    to speak your gospel of love.

Passing the Peace of Christ (Luke 4, 1 Corinthians 13)
Christ comes with words of love and peace. The message is not for a few, but for all people. Love comes to us and brings us peace. Let us share this peace with one another.

✗ Prayer of Preparation (Jeremiah 1, 1 Corinthians 13)
God of grace,
    open our spirits to hear your call;
    open our hearts to receive your love;
    open our mouths to speak your word.
May we trust your wisdom and seek your guidance
    as we hear your words of truth. Amen.

Response to the Word (Jeremiah 1)
God of love,
    you call us to move beyond our comfort zone.
We aren't sure we're ready to do your work.
The tasks seem so big,
    and we feel so small.
Be with us, O God,
    as we respond to your call.
Touch our lips,
    that we may speak your words of love.
Touch our hearts,
    that we may plant your seeds of hope.
Touch our hands,
    that we may serve one another in your name.
Amen.

Response to the Word (1 Corinthians 13)
God of love,
    we don't see things clearly;
    we don't understand the mystery
        of your presence in our lives.
Yet you know us fully—

you understand our struggles,
and believe in our gifts.
May we place our trust in you
and in our love for one another,
that all the world
may rejoice in your love. Amen.

THANKSGIVING AND COMMUNION

Invitation to the Offering
God is our hope and our refuge. God gives us the mysterious gift of love

✗ Offering Prayer (Jeremiah 1, Psalm 71, 1 Corinthians 13)
God of love,
you protect us and comfort us;
you call us on new adventures;
you bless us with your love.
We bring these gifts, and we bring our lives,
as offerings of our love.
Teach us to hope in all things,
to be faithful to you,
and to be known by our love
in everything we do. Amen.

Great Thanksgiving (Jeremiah 1, 1 Corinthians 13, Luke 4)
In the beginning, you called all that is into being.
Your love broke forth,
summoning creation to your vision of peace.
When we failed you—rejoicing in wrongdoing,
boasting of our own power—
you sent prophets to call us back to you.
Your righteousness tears down everything
that hinders your grace—
pulling down structures that oppress,
destroying cruelty, overthrowing injustice.
You built a new way of living, planting seeds of hope
that grow for the healing of creation.

We join with all creation, praising you continually:
Holy, holy, holy Lord, God of power and might,
heaven and earth are full of your glory.
Hosanna in the highest! Blessed is the one
who comes in the name of the Lord.
Hosanna in the highest!

You sent Jesus to walk the paths of love in our midst:
teaching us the ways of justice and truth,
healing our brokenness, speaking your wisdom.
He reached out beyond his own community,
carrying your grace into the wider world.
Through him you gave us the gift of love—
love that bears, believes, hopes,
and endures all things.

Jesus gathered at the table with his companions.
He took the bread, gave thanks to you,
and shared it with his friends.
This is the bread of life; this is the offering of love.
Let us remember Jesus.
At the end of the meal, Jesus took the cup,
gave thanks to you, and shared it with his friends.
This is the cup of joy; this is the offering of love.
Let us remember Jesus.

And as we remember, we offer our lives to the one
whose name is Love, rejoicing in Christ's gift to us.
Christ has died.
Christ is risen.
Christ will come again.

Send forth your Spirit upon us, O God.
Touch our lips with your power.
Touch our hearts with your love,
that we may be the body of Christ, love incarnate.
Pour out your Spirit on these gifts of bread and wine,

that they may be the presence of Christ in our lives,
nourishing us for the work of love.
Through Jesus Christ, and the Holy Spirit
in your holy church, we praise you continually,
Almighty God. Amen.

SENDING FORTH

Benediction (Jeremiah 1, 1 Corinthians 13)
God has put words in your mouths.
God has put love in your hearts.
Go forth to speak God's words of love to the world.
May faith, hope, and love abide with you forever.

CONTEMPORARY OPTIONS

Contemporary Gathering Words (Jeremiah 1)
God calls to us.
> **We're reluctant.**
God calls to us.
> **We doubt our ability.**
God calls to us.
> **We just aren't sure.**
God calls to us and equips us to serve.
> **We're here, Lord.**
> **We're ready.**

Praise Sentences (Psalm 71, Luke 4)
God, you are my rock, my refuge, and my fortress!
The words of Jesus are gracious, amazing the heart!
Love is greatest of all!

Litany (1 Corinthians 13)
Why won't he finish the job?
> **Love is patient.**
I don't like her at all.
> **Love is kind.**
He always gets the best of everything.
> **Love is not envious.**

I can do this better by myself.
   Love is not boastful.
Go away and quit bothering me!
   Love is not rude.
Why won't they do what I want!
   Love does not insist on its own way.
She always gets to me by doing that.
   Love is not irritable.
Why do they always get chosen?
   Love is not envious.
I can't go on like this!
   Love bears all things.
I'm just not sure.
   Love believes all things
Things will never get better.
   Love hopes all things.
I'm ready to give up!
   Love endures all things.
Lord, teach me to love.
   The greatest of these is love.

FEBRUARY 10, 2013

Transfiguration Sunday
Terri Stewart

COLOR
White

SCRIPTURE READINGS
Exodus 34:29-35; Psalm 99; 2 Corinthians 3:12–4:2; Luke 9:28-36 (37-43a)

THEME IDEAS
In the early Semitic view of creation, there was a dome over the earth separating the heavens from the worldly realm. The highest point, the mountaintop, was both the throne and footstool of God. It was here that people went to be with God, to communicate with and receive divine responses. In today's scriptures, both Moses and Jesus go to the mountaintop to communicate intimately with the divine. The psalmist reminds us that we too are to go up the mountain. Likewise, Paul encourages us to see the glory of God and to have mountaintop experiences of God. In all cases, however, we must come down from the mountain and live a life of bold worship and obedience to God in community.

INVITATION AND GATHERING

Call to Worship (Exodus 34, Psalm 99,
2 Corinthians 3–4)
God is mighty!
See the glory of the Lord.

God is forgiving!
See the glory of the Lord.
God is merciful!
See the glory of the Lord.
God is present!
See the glory of the Lord.

Opening Prayer (Exodus 34, Psalm 99, 2 Corinthians 3–4, Luke 9)

Revealing God, Creator of the mountain,
    you have shown your glory to us,
        that we may be transformed.
Help us be bold and strong of heart—
    a holy and righteous people
        who reflect your divine image. Amen.

PROCLAMATION AND RESPONSE

Prayer of Confession (Exodus 34, Psalm 99, 2 Corinthians 3–4)

Merciful God,
    we have been mute
        when you called for boldness;
    we have lost heart
        when you asked for strength;
    we have faltered
        when you demanded justice;
    we have turned away
        when you showed us your truth;
    we have been faithless
        when you cried for fidelity of purpose.
Strengthen our hearts
    as we put away secret shames.
Strengthen our will
    as we practice justice.
Strengthen our mind
    as we cling to truth revealed in Christ Jesus.
We glorify and extol your love forever. Amen.

Words of Assurance (Psalm 99, Luke 9)
Our God is a forgiving God!
When we cry to God, God answers.
In the name of Christ,
   we are healed of our sins.
Receive the forgiveness of God.

Passing the Peace of Christ (Exodus 34, Psalm 99, Luke 9)
The glory of God is mirrored in your face when you speak words of peace and justice. Turn to one another and share signs of this peace, that all may all be transformed by Christ's love.

Response to the Word or Benediction (Exodus 34, Psalm 99, Luke 9)
God of justice and equity,
   we receive your holy words
      with hope for a transformed heart—
         a heart that seeks justice and healing.
Help us be transformed like Christ,
   into witness, healer, and teacher.
Send us down from the mountaintop
   to go forth into the world,
      shining your glory for all to see. Amen.

THANKSGIVING AND COMMUNION

Offering Prayer (Exodus 34, Luke 9)
Gracious God,
   you have loved us so deeply
      and given us so much
         that we cannot help but praise you.
Take these humble gifts
   and transform them for your purposes,
      that together we may bring your radiant love
         to the world. Amen.

Invitation to Communion (Luke 9)

Jesus sat and ate with his friends many times.
Perhaps when preparing to climb the mountain
 where he was transfigured with Moses and Elijah,
 they gathered for a meal together.
Surely, when they gathered,
 they were intimate friends,
 brothers sharing a meal.
And when they broke bread together,
 they strengthened Christ
 for his transformation,
 as only friends can do.
Friends, this table is prepared
 with bread and fruit of the vine
 for the transformation of the world.
Come, let us break bread together.

SENDING FORTH

Benediction (Exodus 34, Psalm 99, Luke 9)

May Christ's love transform you.
 We shine with God's love.
May the joy of God's grace sustain you.
 We shine with Christ's joy.
May you descend from the mountaintop
with boldness to do God's will.
 We shine with the Spirit's power.
Shalom and Amen.

CONTEMPORARY OPTIONS

Contemporary Gathering Words (Luke 9)

A cloud came upon the disciples on that day long ago.
 Listen for the voice of God.
God spoke of the Son, the chosen one.
 Listen for the word of God.
God speaks to us still.
 Listen for the voice of God.

Praise Sentences *(Exodus 34, Psalm 99, Luke 9)*
Holy is God!
We tremble with joy!
Mighty is God!
We tremble with joy!
Radiant is God!
We tremble with joy!

—OR—

Praise Sentences *(Exodus 34, Luke 9)*
Shine, Jesus, shine!
You light up our darkness.
Shine, Jesus, shine!
You light up our lives.
Shine, Jesus, shine!
Shine, Jesus, shine!
Shine, Jesus, shine!
(B. J. Beu)

FEBRUARY 13, 2013

Ash Wednesday
Laura Jaquith Bartlett

COLOR
Purple or Gray

SCRIPTURE READINGS
Joel 2:1-2, 12-17; Psalm 51:1-17; 2 Corinthians 5:20b–6:10;
Matthew 6:1-6, 16-21

THEME IDEAS
Ash Wednesday is typically a time for somber reflection
on our mortality and sinfulness. As such, the scriptures
for the day point to the shortcomings of humanity and our
urgent need to return to God. And yet, this time of worship is not about beating ourselves up or wearing sackcloth and ashes in order to avert God's impending wrath.
The real message of Ash Wednesday is one of hope. If we
offer our hearts to God, whose unlimited mercy and love
are ready and waiting, God receives us with open arms.

INVITATION AND GATHERING

Call to Worship (Joel 2)
Gather the people, young and old.
The day of the Lord is coming.
Blow the trumpet!
The day of the Lord is coming.

"Return to me with all your heart," says the Lord.
The day of the Lord is coming.
It is coming near.

Opening Prayer (Joel 2, Psalm 51, 2 Corinthians 5)

Gracious and merciful God,
we gather in your name on this holy day.
May our hearts return to you
as we begin the season of Lent.
When we struggle with sorrow,
remind us of the joy of your amazing love.
When we focus on the things we lack,
remind us of your limitless generosity.
When we think that we have nothing,
remind us that through the sacrifice of your Son,
we possess everything we truly need.
Take our hearts and make them clean, O God.
Take our lives and make them your own. Amen.

PROCLAMATION AND RESPONSE

Prayer of Confession (Psalm 51)

God, we come before you in our need.
Have mercy on us, O God.
Wipe away the record of our failings.
We are all too aware of the times we have fallen short.
Have mercy on us, O God.
Wash our lives with your forgiveness.
In the midst of our guilt and despair,
grant us the courage to return to you.
Have mercy on us, O God.
Hide your face from our wrongdoing.
Longing to be restored to your presence,
give us a new and willing spirit, we pray!
Have mercy on us, O God.
Restore to us the joy of your salvation.
Show us the light of your love,
and we will constantly sing your praises.

Have mercy on us, O God.
Open our lips to declare your goodness. Amen.

Words of Assurance (Psalm 51)

God does not want burnt offerings
  as atonement for your sins.
Guilt, punishment, and mourning
  are not what God requires.
Offer God your hearts,
  and God will fill you with the joy
  of your salvation.

Passing the Peace of Christ

We often think of the Lenten journey as a personal and
even somewhat lonely walk with God. But the truth is, as
the body of Christ, these forty days can be an experience
of profound community—a time to draw closer to God
and to one another. As we prepare to embark on this journey, I invite you to offer words of support to your travel-
ing companions. Greet one another with signs of Christ's
peace.

Introduction to the Word (Joel 2, Psalm 51)

Open your ears to hear the trumpet that calls us back to
God. Open your eyes to see the ashes that call us back to
God. Open your souls in prayer to feel the longing that
calls us back to God. Open your hearts once again to the
love that calls us back to God.

Introduction to the Imposition of Ashes (Joel 2, 2 Corinthians 5, Psalm 51)

Even now it is not too late to return to the Lord. When we
come before God with a contrite heart, mercy and love
await us. Now is the acceptable time to offer our hearts to
God. Now is the day of salvation. We cannot wait until
we are worthy to approach the throne. The ashes remind
us that we will never be worthy. But the cross that waits
at the end of this journey proclaims that even imperfect
mortals like us are worthy of God's love and salvation.
Here is the delicious irony: as we wear the ashes of

mortality and sin on our foreheads, we are proclaiming God's victory over these very elements. Truly, now is the acceptable time to offer our hearts to God.

Thanksgiving Over the Ashes

Merciful God,
> you ask us to rend our hearts,
>> not our clothing.

In the dust of these ashes,
> we come face-to-face
>> with the shortcomings of our own humanity.

Help us resist the temptation
> to wash away the dust,
>> for we know that it was from the dust itself
>>> that you created us.

Wash our hearts
> and mark us with ashes on the outside,
>> that we might be made clean on the inside. Amen.

IMPOSITION OF ASHES

(People are invited forward to receive the sign of the cross in ashes with these or similar words:)
Be reconciled to God.

THANKSGIVING AND COMMUNION

Offering Prayer (Matthew 6, Psalm 51)

Merciful God,
> we offer you our financial gifts,
>> not so that we can boast of our generosity,
>>> but so that we may share our wealth
>>>> with those in need;
> we offer you our very lives,
>> not so that we can boast of our humanity,
>>> but so that we may know the joy
>>>> of your salvation.

We pray in the name of Jesus Christ. Amen.

SENDING FORTH

Benediction (Joel 2, 2 Corinthians 5)
Go now, walking with your brothers and sisters
   on the journey to Easter.
Go now, listening for the trumpet
   to announce the day of the Lord
   and the promise of salvation.
Go now, knowing that this is the acceptable time
   to offer your hearts to God.
Go now in peace. Amen.

CONTEMPORARY OPTIONS

Contemporary Gathering Words (Joel 2, Based on THE MESSAGE)
God's Day is coming! God's Judgment is on its way!
But there's good news: It's not too late.
God asks us to change our lives, not just our clothes.
Come back to God and discover extravagant love!

Praise Sentences (Joel 2, Psalm 51)
God is gracious and merciful,
   slow to anger and abounding in steadfast love.
God relents from punishing,
   eager to give us another chance.
God's steadfast love and abundant mercy
   wash away our sins.
Praise be to God!

FEBRUARY 17, 2013

First Sunday in Lent

Matthew J. Packer

COLOR

Purple

SCRIPTURE READINGS

Deuteronomy 26:1-11; Psalm 91:1-2, 9-16; Romans 10:8b-13; Luke 4:1-13

THEME IDEAS

As we enter the season of Lent, we enter a time of self-examination and repentance, a time of preparation for the transforming power of Easter. Today's scriptures focus on God's provision and God's protection. In Luke's Gospel, Jesus alludes to Deuteronomy 26, and the devil quotes Psalm 91. In the Epistle reading, Jesus assumes the role of protector and provider for all who confess that Jesus is Lord and believe in their hearts that God raised Jesus from the dead.

INVITATION AND GATHERING

Call to Worship (Psalm 91)

You who live in the shelter of the Most High,
who abide in the shadow of the Almighty,
say to the Lord:
You are my refuge and my fortress.

You are my God in whom I trust.
Because you have made the Lord your refuge,
the Most High will be your dwelling place.
No evil shall befall us.
No scourge shall come near our tents.
Those who love the Lord, God will deliver.
God protects those who know the name of the Lord.
God saves them and honors them in times of trouble.
Show us our salvation, O God.
Show us your favor as we offer you our worship.

Opening Prayer (Romans 10, Psalm 91, Deuteronomy 26, Luke 4)
In the quiet of this moment,
    in the stillness of this place,
        draw near to us, O God.
As we seek the shelter of your refuge,
    as we celebrate the bounty of your provision,
        hearken to our need, Holy One.
Transform this time and place
    into our land of milk and honey—
        a land where you are among us,
        a land where your mighty hand
            and your outstretched arm
                protect us,
        a land where you alone are worthy
            of our worship and service.
We ask this in the saving name of Jesus, our Lord.
Amen.

PROCLAMATION AND RESPONSE

Prayer of Confession (Luke 4, Deuteronomy 26)
Holy Lord,
    as we enter this Lenten season,
        we are reminded of our weakness
        and our need for your strength.

We ask your forgiveness
    when we succumb to the temptations of this world,
        when we tread paths
            that are contrary to your will.
We ask your forgiveness
    when we fail to look beyond our own desires
        to see another's need.
We ask for your presence
    in our wilderness wanderings.
May your hand guide us from the arid land of sin
    into a land flowing with milk and honey—
        a land made rich and abundant
            by your saving love. Amen.

Words of Assurance (Romans 10)
No one who believes in Jesus will be put to shame.
And everyone who calls on the name of the Lord
    shall be saved.
Rejoice and celebrate, for forgiveness is ours
    through the confession of faith in Christ.

Passing the Peace of Christ (Romans 10:9)
Joyously greet one another with the words, "Jesus is
Lord!"

Introduction to the Word or Prayer of Preparation (Deuteronomy 26:8, Romans 10:8)
God of signs and wonders,
    who speaks the world into being,
    speak again your words of life and death.
May your word be ever near us,
    on our lips, and in our heart.
Transform us as we hear your word this day,
    that we may respond with faithful praise. Amen.

Response to the Word
O God,
    you have spoken to us today
        through this word of faith.
Embolden our spirits by your Spirit,

that your words may be made manifest
   in all that we say and in all that we do
     to bring your kingdom on earth.
In the name of Christ, we pray. Amen.

THANKSGIVING AND COMMUNION

Invitation to the Offering (Deuteronomy 26:1-2)
Hear the word of the Lord:
   "When you have come into the land
   that the LORD your God is giving you...
   you shall take some of the first of
   all the fruit of the ground...
   and go to the place that the LORD your God will choose
   as a dwelling [place]."
We bring our best before God in recognition
that all that we have is an inheritance from God.
In celebration of the bounty that God has provided,
let us give generously as we collect today's offering.

Offering Prayer (Deuteronomy 26)
We bring these gifts to you, O God,
   in recognition and gratitude
     for your loving provision.
We offer you our very lives and bow before you
   in tribute to your many blessings.
Take us and use us,
   that your will may be done on earth
     as it is in heaven.
This we pray in the name of the One
   who came in holy love,
     that we might have abundant life. Amen.

SENDING FORTH

Benediction (Psalm 91:9-12)
God will command the angels concerning you
to guard you in all your ways.
On their hands they will bear us up.

Because you have made the Lord your refuge,
the Most High will be your dwelling place.
No evil shall befall us.
Go in peace, in the provision and protection
of the Lord.
Thanks be to God! Amen.

CONTEMPORARY OPTIONS

Contemporary Gathering Words (Romans 10)
Call upon our God,
for God will hear our cry!
Calling, you will be saved,
for God will hear our cry!
In confidence and faith,
come and gather in the protective love of God,
for God will hear our cry!

Praise Sentences (Psalm 91:1-2)
You who live in the shelter of the Most High,
who abide in the shadow of the Almighty,
say to the Lord, "My refuge and my fortress;
my God, in you I trust!"
My God, in you I trust!

FEBRUARY 24, 2013

Second Sunday in Lent

B. J. Beu

COLOR

Purple

SCRIPTURE READINGS

Genesis 15:1-12, 17-18; Psalm 27; Philippians 3:17–4:1; Luke 13:31-35

THEME IDEAS

Stark contrasts weave these texts together: darkness and light, death and salvation, shame and glory, betrayal and fidelity. In terrifying darkness, God enters into a covenant with Abram; yet, the psalmist proclaims God to be our light and our salvation. Adversaries rise against us in war, but God saves the faithful, turning fear into shouts of joy. Philippians warns that enemies of Christ revel in shame, while true disciples shine in God's glory. And Jesus brushes off warnings about Herod's plan to kill him because nothing will deter him from doing the works of God: healing the sick, preaching the good news, casting out demons. Today's readings provide rich imagery depicting the choices we face in our faith journey—choices that have consequences for us and for our world.

INVITATION AND GATHERING

Call to Worship (Psalm 27)
The Lord is our light and our salvation,
whom shall we fear?
Though adversaries encamp against us,
God conceals and protects us from harm.
Though enemies seek to bring us low,
God lifts us up to stand on higher ground.
Sing to the Lord with songs of joy.
Make melody to the Lord, our God.
The Lord is our light and our salvation,
whom shall we fear?

Opening Prayer (Genesis 15, Psalm 27, Philippians 3)
Mysterious One,
in terrifying darkness
you descended to Abram while he slept.
In the secret place of our dreams,
in the darkest night of our fears,
you come to us
and overshadow us,
filling us with hope and dread.
Your power draws us like a moth to the flame.
Hear us when we cry out to you, O God.
Be our light and our salvation.
Teach us the ways of heaven,
that we may be children of your promise. Amen.

PROCLAMATION AND RESPONSE

Prayer of Confession (1 Corinthians 12)
Gracious God,
we would rather warn your servants
when they are in danger,
than join them in their work:
healing the sick and offering good news
to the downtrodden;

we would rather bask in the light
of your salvation,
than journey into the darkness of self-discovery,
standing naked before you
with all of our faults exposed;
we would rather keep our faith
a private affair,
than proclaim boldly for all to hear:
"Blessed is the one who comes
in the name of the Lord."
Find us in the dark, mighty God,
and shine your light upon us,
that we may have the courage
to brave the deepest night
and find others who are lost in the dark.

Words of Assurance (Luke 13)
Christ desires to gather us together,
as a mother hen gathers her brood under her wing.
God's love and mercy pursue us,
even in the darkest night.
Rejoice in the good news of God's forgiveness!
Thanks be to God!

Response to the Word (Genesis 15, Psalm 27)
God's mercy leads us into terrifying darkness,
healing our weaknesses
and shining the light of love
into the shadows of our lives.
God is the light of our salvation,
securing us a heritage in Christ's name.
God does not leave us in ignorance,
but teaches us the ways of life and death.
Let us choose life.

THANKSGIVING AND COMMUNION

Offering Prayer (Genesis 15, Psalm 27)
God of light,
your blessings are as numerous as the stars;

your mercy is as deep as the sea.
When we had no future,
you blessed us with a heritage that endures.
When we fall prey to our adversaries,
you lift us up to stand safely on higher ground.
In thanksgiving and praise for your many gifts,
we offer you our tithes and offerings,
that through these gifts,
others may dwell in the land of the living
and know your goodness.

SENDING FORTH

Benediction (Isaiah 62, Psalm 36)
The Lord is our light and our salvation.
In God, we are not afraid.
The Lord is our fortress and rock
that shelters us from the storm.
In God we dwell secure.
The Lord is our resting place,
gathering us together as a mother hen
gathers her brood under her wing.
In God we find our true home.
Go with the blessings of the One
who leads us into terrifying darkness
to fill our lives with light and hope.

CONTEMPORARY OPTIONS

Contemporary Gathering Words (Psalm 27)
God is our light and our salvation.
Whom shall we fear?
God is our light and our salvation.
What is there to be afraid of?
God is our light and our salvation.
Laugh and sing to the Lord.
God is our light and our salvation.
Thanks be to God!

Praise Sentences (Psalm 27)
God's light is shining.
   Sing and shout to the Lord.
God's light is shining.
   Rejoice and be glad!
God's light is shining.
   Dance and reach to the heavens.
God's light is shining.
   God's light is shining.
God's light is shining.

MARCH 3, 2013

Third Sunday in Lent
Mary J. Scifres

COLOR
Purple

SCRIPTURE READINGS
Isaiah 55:1-9; Psalm 63:1-8; 1 Corinthians 10:1-13; Luke 13:1-9

THEME IDEAS
The soul yearns for many types of nourishment as we hunger and thirst for God. Today's focus is on the hunger and thirst for grace. In the Lenten season, we return to God, not simply to get recentered and refocused, but to acknowledge our desperate desire for the health and wholeness we find in Christ. The thirst for grace propels us forward, satisfying us like nothing else can. Surely, this is the bread of heaven, the manna that feeds the spirit, the living water that quenches the soul. Come to the waters of grace. Receive the wine of salvation and the milk of God's teachings, offered without money or price. Come and eat the goodness of Christ's grace, God's steadfast love, and the Spirit's abundant acceptance.

INVITATION AND GATHERING

Call to Worship (Isaiah 55, Psalm 63, 1 Corinthians 10, Luke 13)
Come to the waters of grace.
Here, our thirst is satisfied.

Come to the rivers of love.
Here, our parched mouths sing with praise.
Come to the tree bearing the fruit of life.
Here, our hungry souls are fed.
Come to the One who loves us.
Here, our hearts find joy,
our spirits reside in deepest love.
Come to the waters of grace.
Here, our thirst is satisfied.

Opening Prayer or Communion Prayer (Isaiah 55, Psalm 63, 1 Corinthians 10)

God of grace and God of glory,
pour out your Spirit upon all of us gathered here,
that we may be washed in the spirit of your love
and fed with the bread of your teachings.
Open our hearts,
that we may truly accept your abundant grace
and steadfast love.
As our souls reach to you in this time of worship,
embrace us with your love.
In Christ's name, we pray. Amen.

PROCLAMATION AND RESPONSE

Prayer of Confession (Isaiah 55, Psalm 63, Luke 13)

Merciful God, full of grace,
hear our prayer of confession and need.
(Silence may follow.)
As we hunger for forgiveness,
feed us with your grace.
As we thirst for righteousness,
fill us with your mercy,
that we may be merciful and just
as your disciples upon this earth.
As we faint from the aridness
of mistakes that haunt us and sins that destroy us,
lift us from despair into newness of life.

Hold our hands, lift us up, and clutch us to your breast,
    that we might cling to you with laughter and joy
        in the abundance of your love.
Feed us with your strength and wisdom,
    that we might bear fruit,
        abundant with love and justice,
            for a world in need. Amen.

Words of Assurance (Isaiah 55, 1 Corinthians 10)
Come to the waters,
    you who are thirsty for grace and forgiveness.
For grace is Christ's gift to us,
    offered without money or price.
Drink from the wellspring of salvation,
    that you may know God's mercy
    and revel in the living waters of Christ's love.
Come to the waters,
    for in these waters of grace, you are forgiven!

Passing the Peace of Christ (1 Corinthians 10)
Do not destroy one another with complaints, Paul advises.
Rather, share the spiritual drink that is Christ's love, given
to and for all. Share signs of this love with one another as
we pass the peace of Christ—the peace that passes all
understanding, the peace that mends all broken hearts.

Response to the Word (Isaiah 55, Psalm 63, Luke 13)
As we reflect on a world hungry for God's love,
    let us be fruit-bearing trees,
    flowering with kindness and compassion.
As we remember those who thirst for forgiveness,
    let us be life-giving waters,
    flowing with mercy and grace.
As we remember our own parched souls,
    let us cling to God and God's people,
    that we may find an oasis of steadfast love.
Let us pray.
    Merciful God, full of grace,
    live in us and flow through us,

that we may be an oasis of steadfast love
in all that we say, in all that we do,
and in all that we are.
In Christ's grace, we pray. Amen.

THANKSGIVING AND COMMUNION

Invitation to the Offering (Isaiah 55, Luke 13)

Come to the waters. Share from the abundance in your
life, that others may taste of God's grace and be washed in
the living water of Christ's love.

Offering Prayer (Isaiah 55, Psalm 63, Luke 13)

God of abundant love,
we thank you for your abundant gifts
as we return a portion of those gifts back to you.
Tend the roots of our lives,
that we may continue to bear much fruit.
Tend the shoots of this church,
that we may be a forest filled with life-giving fruit
and haven-like shade
for a world hungering for your love
and desperate for your protection.
In gratitude, we pray. Amen.

Invitation to Communion

Come to the bread of life,
all who hunger for love.
Come to the living water,
all who thirst for righteousness.
Come to the shelter of God,
all who face danger and persecution
Come to the shade of Christ's love,
all who suffer sorrow and grief.
Come to the Lamb of God,
all who need mercy and grace.
Come to the table of love,
all who yearn for the abundant gifts of God,
offered in Christ and the Holy Spirit.

Great Thanksgiving (Isaiah 55, Lent)
Lift up your hearts!
    We lift them up to God!
Let us give thanks to Yahweh, our God.
    It is right to give our thanks and praise.

We give thanks and praise to you,
    O Bread of Life!
We give thanks for your abundant creation,
    called forth in ancient times upon this earth,
    and manifested in your grace
    when you created us in your very image.
From ancient times, you have fed us, nourished us,
    and strengthened our souls for this journey.
In the days of wandering in the wilderness,
    in the songs of psalmists,
    and in the harsh wisdom of the prophets,
    you have offered us the water of righteousness
    and the bread of justice.
(Sanctus may be sung or spoken here.)

In the fullness of time,
    you came to us in the presence of Jesus Christ—
    the bread of abundant life, eternal, living water.
Even when facing death,
    Christ gave thanks and blessed the fruit of this,
    your good earth, offering not only bread and wine,
    but the bread that always satisfies
    and life that never ends.
We remember Christ's grace-filled words:
    "Take, eat, this is my body, broken for you.
    Take, drink. This is my life poured out for you
    and for many, for the forgiveness of sins."

As we walk this journey of life,
    we remember these gifts
    as we proclaim the mystery of faith.

Christ has died.
Christ is risen.
Christ will come again.

Grant us your grace, and shower your Spirit
 upon these gifts.
Transform this bread into the mercy
 for which we hunger.
Create in this sacrament the new wine of grace
 for which we thirst.
Create in us a new community of abundant love,
 that we may be life-giving disciples of Christ,
 one with each other,
 one in unity with you through the Holy Spirit,
 and one in ministry to a world
 that hungers for your grace and mercy.
(Words of acclamation may be offered here.)
Amen.

SENDING FORTH

Benediction (Isaiah 55, Luke 13)
 Let God dig a little more in the garden of your lives,
 trusting that there is yet much fruit
 for the Spirit to bring forth.
 We go forth with the confidence
 that Christ's abounding love
 is sufficient for the day.
 As children fed by God's grace
 and watered with Christ's mercy,
 go forth to feed a world in need.
 We go forth with trust and hope,
 rejoicing in God's glorious grace!

CONTEMPORARY OPTIONS

Contemporary Gathering Words (Isaiah 55, Psalm 63,
1 Corinthians 10)
 Are you hungry and thirsty
 for more than just food and drink?

Do you yearn for the bread that truly satisfies?
Come, all you who thirst.
Come, all you who hunger.
Christ is present here—
    bread for the journey, living water for the soul.
Come and taste the nourishing gift of God's grace.

Praise Sentences (Psalm 63)

Behold, the power of love!
Rejoice in the miracle of grace!
    We behold the power of love!
    We rejoice in the miracle of grace!

MARCH 10, 2013

Fourth Sunday in Lent
Rebecca J. Kruger Gaudino

COLOR
Purple

SCRIPTURE READINGS
Joshua 5:9-12; Psalm 32; 2 Corinthians 5:16-21;
Luke 15:1-3, 11b-32

THEME IDEAS
Today's readings speak of the power of honest human
speech, heard and answered by a God who delivers us from
burden and bondage to freedom and possibility. These readings testify that even before we speak, God, as loving parent,
waits for the wandering child; God, as provider, gives
manna even while we wander. God waits on us, listens for
us, plans for us, and reaches out to us most compellingly in
Jesus Christ. Our texts instruct us to speak our deepest failings and fears, for to be silent, to hold everything within, is
to waste away. When we speak boldly and honestly, we hear
God's glad cry: "Quickly, bring out a robe!"

INVITATION AND GATHERING

Call to Worship (Psalm 32, 2 Corinthians 5:16-21)
In Jesus Christ, there is a new creation.
Everything old has passed away.
Everything has become new.

This newness is from God,
who has reconciled us through Jesus Christ.
Rejoice and be glad!
Everything has become new.

Opening Prayer

God of steadfast love and mercy,
    remind us once again that in Jesus Christ
        everything has become new.
For far too often,
    things seem as they have always been:
        old habits die hard,
        difficult situations linger,
        failures from our past linger.
We look for your promised newness
    but cannot see it.
Speak to us again of your new creation.
Open our eyes to its presence in our lives.
Call us forth to claim this newness,
    that we may be healed and made whole. Amen.

PROCLAMATION AND RESPONSE

Prayer of Confession (Psalm 32)

O God,
        when we keep silence about our sin,
        we waste away with regret and guilt;
        we feel your hand upon us,
            and our strength dries up.
And so we acknowledge our sin to you,
        holding nothing back,
            for you are a hiding place for us;
            we trust in you to preserve us.
Forgive us and reclaim us, we pray. Amen.

Words of Assurance (Psalm 32)

Steadfast love surrounds those
        who put their trust in God,
            for God forgives the guilt of their sin.

Happy are those whose transgression is forgiven!
Be glad in God!

Prayer of Preparation (Psalm 32)

O God,
>teach us the way that we should go;
>counsel us in the ways of life.

We wait upon your teaching and counsel,
>for we are lost without it. Amen.

Response to the Word (Luke 15)

(Use this as a Prayer of Confession after a sermon based on Luke 15)
Loving Parent, Mother, Father God,
>when we wander to distant places,
>>you watch the road to greet us
>>>when we finally come home.

Whenever we are far from you,
>remind us that we are your beloved children,
>>the longing of your heart,
>>>and give us the strength and courage
>>>>to return to your open arms.

When we have sinned against heaven and before you,
>forgive us, for we are coming home! Amen.

Words of Assurance (Luke 15)

Quickly, bring out the robes, the best ones.
Put them on—and these golden rings, too!
For my children who were lost are now found.
Let us celebrate and rejoice!
*(Hobby shops sell very inexpensive, bendable rings. Drape a
luxurious robe on the Communion table, and pass out baskets of
golden rings to joyous music.)*

—OR—

Response to the Word or Benediction (Psalm 32)

Happy are those whose sin is forgiven!
In times of distress,
>the mighty waters shall not reach us.

You, O God, are our hiding place.

You preserve us from trouble.
You surround us with glad cries of deliverance.
Happy are those whose sin is forgiven!

THANKSGIVING AND COMMUNION

Invitation to the Offering (Luke 15, 2 Corinthians 5)
Through the gifts of our possessions and our presence, we
let those who are far from home know that we are their
brothers and sisters. Through our gifts, we welcome them
to our home, to God's home. We are the ambassadors for
Jesus, our brother and savior, spreading the news of a
home of love and hope through our gifts.

Offering Prayer (Luke 15)
Bless these gifts, Generous God,
    that they may be used to find your children—
        children who wander in hunger,
        children who long to come home.
Through our gifts,
    may all who wander set off for home,
    and may we celebrate and rejoice
        in their homecoming. Amen.

SENDING FORTH

Benediction (Psalm 32, Luke 15)
Go forth in renewed strength, knowing who you are:
    the sons and daughters of God—
    celebrated, rejoiced in, welcomed, dearly loved.
Wear your robe and ring with joy!
Be glad in God and rejoice, O you righteous!

CONTEMPORARY OPTIONS

Contemporary Gathering Words (Psalm 32, 2 Corinthians 5, Luke 15)
Have you looked for crocus shoots or buds on trees?
Look around and see the newness!

Did you hear this week about love in action?
Look around and see the newness!
Did someone who was lost find her way home?
Look around and see the newness!
In Jesus Christ, God is busy making all things new!
Be glad in God and rejoice!

Praise Sentences (Psalm 32)
Be glad in God and rejoice!
Everything old has passed away!
Be glad in God and rejoice!
Everything has become new!

MARCH 17, 2013

Fifth Sunday in Lent

Kate Cudlipp

COLOR

Purple

SCRIPTURE READINGS

Isaiah 43:16-21; Psalm 126; Philippians 3:4b-14;
John 12:1-8

THEME IDEAS

Lent confronts us with our propensity to hold onto old habits and self-serving beliefs. Today's scriptures call us to be willing to experience the sorrow of loss, as we leave behind familiar, comfortable lives to join Jesus on the arduous path to new, joyful life in God.

INVITATION AND GATHERING

Call to Worship (Isaiah 43, Psalm 126, John 12)
The days ahead are dark and full of foreboding.
    We watch as Jesus journeys to the cross.
There is no way to change what is to come.
    Yet death has not the final word.
Let us bear witness to God's new life
moving within and among us.
    God is doing a new thing.
    Let us rejoice and give thanks!

Opening Prayer (John 12)

Holy Sustainer,
  you were ever in and with Jesus
    on his journey to Jerusalem,
      guiding his choices
        and strengthening his courage
          each step of the way.
As your beloved children,
  be with us and strengthen us on our journeys.
Through our time of worship
  and our companionship with one another,
    teach us to recognize Christ
      in everyone we meet.
Help us offer holy hospitality wherever it is needed,
  and free us from our fears of scarcity,
    that we may share from our abundance
      and be a blessing for others. Amen.

PROCLAMATION AND RESPONSE

Prayer of Confession (Isaiah 43, Psalm 126, Philippians 3)

Holy Source of New Life,
  you promise to set us free
    from paths of fear, doubt, and denial.
  Yet we resist your invitation,
    seeing only what we must give up
      if we are to follow the path of Jesus.
You call us to have faith
  in your sustaining presence and power,
  but your call takes us beyond
    anything we can see or touch.
  We fear placing our trust
    in things beyond our control.
We doubt that you can bring water
  to the dry places of our lives
    or replace our suffering with joy.

Forgive us when we turn away
from your promise of abundant life.
Heal us and lead us home, Holy One. Amen.

Words of Assurance (Philippians 3)
Whenever we seek to leave behind our old ways
  and turn to God for help,
  God forgives our faithlessness
  and strengthens us for the journey ahead.
We are the heirs of God's promises.
We are the children of God's compassion and mercy.

Passing the Peace of Christ
As we resolve to follow the path that Jesus walked, let us
offer one another the sustaining power of Christ's peace.
The peace of Christ be with you, always.
And also with you.

Response to the Word (Psalm 126, Philippians 3)
Eternal Source of Truth,
  free us from the claims of false gods
    and show us the way to lasting joy.
We know the way will not be easy,
  but your word sustains us.
May your good news take root within us,
  that our lives might bear witness
    to the triumph of love over fear,
      and life over death. Amen.

THANKSGIVING AND COMMUNION

Offering Prayer (Psalm 126, John 12)
Faithful Giver of Life,
  you have done great things for us.
In the life and teaching of your Son Jesus,
  you welcome us into your heart.
Help us open our hearts to others,
  that we may be ever more willing
    to offer our hospitality, our support,

and our material resources
wherever they are needed.
Bless these offerings in your holy name. Amen.

SENDING FORTH

Benediction (Isaiah 43, Psalm 126, Philippians 3)
We leave this gathering,
knowing that Christ Jesus
has made us his own.
Take the fruits of our worship into the world,
bringing joy to those who weep,
welcome to the outcast,
and comfort to those who grieve.
God is doing a new thing.
Thanks be to God.

CONTEMPORARY OPTIONS

Contemporary Gathering Words (Isaiah 43, Psalm 126, Philippians 3)
Jesus is on the road to Jerusalem.
We watch in sorrow.
God promises, "I am about to do a new thing."
We wait in hope.
God is faithful.
Our tears will turn to shouts of joy.

Praise Sentences (Philippians 3)
Christ Jesus has made us his own!
Thanks be to God!

MARCH 24, 2013

Palm/Passion Sunday

B. J. Beu

COLOR

Purple

PALM SUNDAY READINGS

Psalm 118:1-2, 19-29; Luke 19:28-40

PASSION SUNDAY READINGS

Isaiah 50:4-9a; Psalm 31:9-16; Philippians 2:5-11; Luke 22:14–23:56 or Luke 23:1-49

THEME IDEAS

After the initial joy of Jesus coming into Jerusalem like a king, fickleness of heart and betrayal are themes of the day. Shortly after singing Jesus' praises as he rode a colt into the holy city, the crowds and even his disciples betrayed and denied him. To avoid moving from the joy of Palm Sunday to the joy of Easter without moving through the anguish of Holy Thursday and Good Friday, today's service focuses on the all-too-human trait of falling away when we should be following faithfully.

INVITATION AND GATHERING

Call to Worship (Psalm 118)

(Begin service with a bare altar/Lord's Table. The words in reduced type are read offstage.)

When they had come near Bethphage and Bethany,
at the place called the Mount of Olives,
Jesus sent two of his disciples ahead, saying to them,
"Go into the village ahead of you, and as you
enter it you will find tied there a colt that has
never been ridden. Untie it and bring it here. If
anyone asks you, 'Why are you untying it?' just
say this, 'The Lord has need of it.'"
This is the day that the Lord has made.
Let us rejoice and be glad in it.
(Church bell, chime, or gong sounds. Have a few youth come
forward and cover the altar with brightly colored cloth as the
words below are read.)
After bringing the colt to Jesus
and throwing their cloaks on its back,
the disciples set Jesus upon it.
As he rode along, people spread their cloaks
upon the road.
The stone that the builders rejected
has become the chief cornerstone.
This is the Lord's doing.
It is marvelous in our eyes.
(Church bell, chime, or gong sounds.)
Open the gates of righteousness, O God,
that we may enter through them.
This is the day that the Lord has made.
Let us rejoice and be glad in it.
(Begin light, joyful music. If you have liturgical dancers, dance.
Light a single Christ Candle or multiple lights as the words
below are read.)
The Lord is God, and God has given us light
as a lamp to our feet.
The light shines in the darkness,
and the darkness has not overcome it.
(Church bell, chime, or gong sounds as music continues to play.)
Bind the festival procession with palm branches.
Enter the gates of righteousness with shouts
of thanksgiving.

**Blessed is the one who comes
in the name of the Lord.
Peace in heaven,
and glory to God in the highest heaven!**
Hearing the crowd's shouts of praise,
some of the Pharisees said to Jesus,
"Teacher, order your disciples to stop."
(Music stops abruptly at the word stop.)
But Jesus answered,
  "I tell you, if these were silent,
  the stones would shout out."
*(Blow a low horn or play an instrument that evokes the sound
of stones crying out.)*
This is the day that the Lord has made.
Let us rejoice and be glad in it!
*(Youth enter and march around the sanctuary as a joyful hymn
such as "All Glory, Laud, and Honor" is sung.)*

Opening Prayer (Luke 22–23, Philippians 2)
Blessed one,
  humbling yourself on the back of a colt,
    you entered Jerusalem in lowly estate
      bring joy to the hearts of children;
    forsaking equality with God,
      you emptied yourself of prestige and power,
        coming as a servant to all.
Sing in our hearts once more,
  that we may remember the joy
    of dancing and singing our hosannas
      like the children of Jerusalem—
        for to such as these
          belong the kingdom of heaven. Amen.

PROCLAMATION AND RESPONSE

Prayer of Confession (Philippians 2, Luke 22–23)
Abiding Spirit,
  your love meets us where we need you most:
    in seasons of doubt;

in periods of weakness;
in moments of betrayal;
in times of denial;
in glimpses of evil disguised as virtue.
Forgive our wayward feet
and our fickle hearts.
Teach us again your ways of life and death,
that we may not stumble and fall
during times of trial.
In your holy name, we pray. Amen.

—*OR*—

Prayer of Confession (Luke 22–23)
God of righteousness,
we would rather sing hosannas
with a cheering crowd,
than stand up for our convictions
in the face of an angry mob;
we would rather dine at your table
with those we call friends,
than admit we are no different
from those we consider enemies.
we would rather view ourselves
as your champions,
than admit how easily
we might betray you with a kiss.
Forgive our fickle faith,
and strengthen our resolve
to be your disciples. Amen.

Words of Assurance (Psalm 118)
Christ has opened the gates of righteousness
and beckons us to walk through.
The stone that the builders rejected
has become the cornerstone of our salvation.
Rejoice and be glad,
for the one who comes in the name of the Lord
has brought us salvation in his name. Amen.

Response to the Word (Isaiah 50, Luke 22–23)
Merciful God,
>your words are like the tongue of a teacher
>>that sustains the weary
>>>and awakens those who slumber.
We love and fear your word, O God—
>we tremble when we think how easily
>>we betray you like Judas;
>we shake when we realize how many times
>>we deny you like Peter.
Put your words of life within our hearts,
>that we may be strengthened to walk with Christ
>>until the bitter end. Amen.

Call to Prayer (Psalm 31)
Like broken vessels,
>we need God's healing.
Like those who are dead,
>we need the stirring of God's Spirit within.
Like an army surrounded by its enemies,
>we need God's protection and deliverance.
Let us lift up our prayers to God,
>for it is the Lord alone
>>who delivers us from evil,
>>who strengthens us to stand,
>>and who makes us whole again.

THANKSGIVING AND COMMUNION

Offering Prayer (Philippians 2, Luke 22–23)
We thank you, O God,
>for your generous Spirit;
>for Christ's gift of self;
>for your never-failing love.
For your many gifts,
>we thank you.
For caring enough to walk with us in our weakness,
>we praise you.

77

Receive these gifts in token and thanks
for the love you offer us,
a love that makes us well and whole. Amen.

SENDING FORTH

Benediction (Psalm 118)
On the back of a donkey,
Jesus came to bless us.
With the light of his love,
Jesus came to illumine our way.
From the power of aimlessness and sin,
Jesus came to set us free.
With the power of the Holy Spirit,
Jesus came to save us.
Go with the blessings of God's anointed.

—OR—

Benediction (Psalm 118)
The gates of righteousness are thrown wide.
Christ has blessed us with life.
The path of salvation is made plain.
Christ has blessed us with truth.
The cornerstone of our faith is sure.
Christ has blessed us with grace.
The gates of righteousness are thrown wide.
Praise be to God!

CONTEMPORARY OPTIONS

Contemporary Gathering Words (Psalm 118)
Jesus is the rock of our salvation.
But the builders rejected that rock.
Jesus is the gate of righteousness.
But so many considered him a fraud.
Jesus has become the cornerstone of our lives.
Can he really be the foundation of our faith?
Come! Let us worship the one

who comes in the name of the Lord.
**We will enter the gate of righteousness
and worship the Lord!**

Praise Sentences (Psalm 118)
This is the day that the Lord has made,
let us rejoice and be glad in it!
Give thanks to the Lord,
for God's steadfast love endures forever.
God's steadfast love endures even now.
This is the day that the Lord has made,
let us rejoice and be glad in it!

MARCH 28, 2013

Holy Thursday
Deborah Sokolove

COLOR
Purple

SCRIPTURE READINGS
Exodus 12:1-4 (5-10) 11-14; Psalm 116:1-4, 12-19;
1 Corinthians 11:23-26; John 13:1-17, 31b-35

THEME IDEAS
As God loves the world, so we are to love one another in
grateful thanks for our salvation from all that holds us in
bondage.

INVITATION AND GATHERING

Call to Worship (John 13)
Jesus calls us to wash one another's feet
and serve one another in love.
   We come to glorify the Holy One.
Jesus invites us to eat and drink with him
and remember him in all that we do.
   We come to the feast with joy.
Jesus commands us to love one another
and show the world that we are his disciples.
   **We come to be the body of Christ
   and know ourselves as his disciples.**

3/22/15

Opening Prayer (Exodus 12, John 13)
God of Moses and Aaron and Miriam,
    when you called the people out of bondage
        in the land of Egypt,
        you commanded them to remember that day
            with feasting and celebration.
When Jesus taught his friends
    to wash one another's feet,
    he commanded them to remember that day
        with love and humble service.
As we remember the last night
    that Jesus shared with his friends,
    help us to glorify you
        and show the world that we are his disciples
            by loving each other and the world.
In the name of Jesus, who is the Christ, we pray.
    Amen.

PROCLAMATION AND RESPONSE

Prayer of Confession (John 13)
Compassionate One,
    your ways lead to life.
You call us to love one another
    and bear one another's burdens.
    But when we disagree with one another,
        we want to be right
            more than we want to follow you.
You call us to serve one another
    and kneel at each other's feet
        in humility and grace.
    But when we are hurt by another,
        we want to strike back
            more than we want to forgive.
You call us to pour out our lives
    for the healing of the world.
    Forgive us for acting

as if your gifts were for us alone,
when you gave up everything,
that all might be blessed
through your sacrifice.

Words of Assurance (Exodus 12, 1 Corinthians 11, John 13)

The God of Exodus and of Calvary
loves us and nourishes us,
feeding us with the bread of compassion
and filling our cups
with an endless stream of grace.
In the name of Christ, we are forgiven.
Thanks be to God. Amen.

Passing the Peace of Christ (John 13)

Remembering Jesus' commandment to love one another,
let us greet one another with signs of peace.
The peace of Christ be with you always.
The peace of Christ be with you always.

Introduction to the Word or Prayer of Preparation (Exodus 12, John 13)

God of memory and hope, God of Exodus and Calvary,
as you led the Israelites into a new life of freedom,
lead us into new life of loving service
as we hear your word.
Fill our hearts with love,
and our minds with understanding. Amen.

Response to the Word (John 13)

God of Moses and Miriam and Aaron,
God of yesterday and tomorrow,
when Jesus washed the feet of his friends,
he taught us how to love one another.
We give you thanks, gracious God,
for leading us out of bondage
to our self-centered lives,
and for feeding us with the bread
of your salvation. Amen.

THANKSGIVING AND COMMUNION

Offering Prayer (1 Corinthians 11)
As Jesus gave himself to us,
in bread broken for us
and in wine poured out for us,
we bring these gifts
for the healing of the world. Amen.

Invitation to Communion
Christ be with you.
And also with you.
Lift up your hearts.
We lift them up to God
Let us give our thanks to the Holy One.
It is right to give our thanks and praise.

It is a right, good, and a joyful thing
always and everywhere to give our thanks to you,
who led the Israelites out of bondage into freedom,
who commanded them to keep the Passover
as a remembrance of how you saved their firstborn
from death, and how you brought them out
of the land of Egypt.

And so, with your creatures on earth
and all the heavenly chorus,
we praise your name
and join their unending hymn, saying:
Holy, holy, holy One, God of power and might,
heaven and earth are full of your glory.
Hosanna in the highest. Blessed is the one
who comes your holy name.
Hosanna in the highest.

Holy are you, and holy is the Lamb of God,
Jesus Christ, who taught us how to love
and serve one another,

and who poured out his life
for the healing of the world.

On the night before his death, Jesus took bread,
gave thanks to you, broke the bread,
gave it to the disciples, saying:
"Take, eat; this is my body which is given for you.
Do this in remembrance of me."
When the supper was over, Jesus took the cup,
offered thanks and gave it to the disciples, saying:
"Drink from this, all of you;
this is my life in the new covenant, poured out
for you and for many, for the forgiveness of sins.
Do this, as often as you drink it,
in remembrance of me."
And so, in remembrance of your mighty acts
in Jesus Christ, we proclaim the mystery of faith.
Christ has died.
Christ is risen.
Christ will come again.

Pour out your Holy Spirit on all of us gathered here,
and on these gifts of bread and wine.
Make them be for us the body and blood of Christ,
that we may be the body of Christ,
in service to all who are oppressed.
God of Moses and Miriam and Aaron,
God of Exodus and Calvary,
God of memory and hope,
we praise your holy, eternal name. Amen.

SENDING FORTH

Benediction (John 13)
Jesus said, "Just as I have loved you,
you also should love one another."
May the God who is love,
fill you with love and compassion,

that everyone may know
you are the followers of Christ.

CONTEMPORARY OPTIONS

Contemporary Gathering Words (John 13)
We come to the feast with joy.
We become what we eat, the body of Christ.

Praise Sentences (Psalm 116)
I will lift up the cup of salvation
and call on the name of the Holy One.
I will pay my vows to the Holy One
in the presence of all God's people.

MARCH 29, 2013

Good Friday

Mary J. Scifres

COLOR
Black or None

SCRIPTURE READINGS
Isaiah 52:13–53:12; Psalm 22; Hebrews 10:16-25;
John 18:1–19:42

THEME IDEAS
On this day, we face what for many is our greatest fear: death. The death of Jesus, the death of hope, and the death of our denial of the reality of death—all these stare us in the face on Good Friday. Simplistic faith and naïve hope come crashing down, as we remember this tragic story, retold over the last two thousand years. This is not a worship service for milk-fed babes, but for those who are open to transformation—those who would allow the words of liturgy and scripture and the music of sacred song to seep into their souls, work through their grief, and invite them to ponder the mystery of tragedy and death. The gift to those who can face Good Friday and endure the emptiness of Holy Saturday is preparation. Facing the truth of Jesus' death prepares us to celebrate mystery and the unexpected joy of Jesus' resurrection.

INVITATION AND GATHERING

Call to Worship (Psalm 22, John 19)

Draw near to God on this day,
a day when God seems so far away.
We cry for help, in need of God's strength.
Remember the story of betrayal and death,
the saddest of our faith.
**We wonder how those who loved him
could have all fallen away.**
Listen and pray on this day of reflection,
seeking to understand death and destruction.
We yearn to know the salvation of God.
Draw near, dear friends,
for God is as near to us as our very breath.
**God was there, hanging on the cross with Jesus,
and God is here with us now.**

Song of Remembrance

"Go to Dark Gethsemane," stanzas 1–3

Opening Prayer (John 18, John 19)

Jesus,
    remember us as we remember you;
    remember us as we remember
      your amazing gift of life
        and your sacrificial love.
Comfort us in our sorrow.
Strengthen us to face the reality of this day—
    death and sin, pain and despair, love and loss.
Invite us into your story once more,
    that we may know how best to follow you—
      all the way to the cross,
      all the way through death,
      all the way to the hope
        on the other side of suffering and death.

Song of Petition

"Jesus, Remember Me"

PROCLAMATION AND RESPONSE

Scripture Reading
John 18:1-27

Call to Confession
"God, How Can We Forgive?"

Prayer of Confession (John 18, John 19)
Forgive us, merciful God, when we deny you
and betray those who seek our welfare.
Lord, have mercy.
Forgive us when we forget your story
and deny your place in our lives.
Christ, have mercy.
Forgive us when we wash our hands of responsibility
and refuse to stand up for truth.
Lord, have mercy.
Forgive us when we follow crowds that would crucify,
when we listen to ideas that destroy.
Kyrie, eleison.
Forgive us when we mock and scorn others,
without listening to their cries of despair.
Christe, eleison.
Forgive us when we deny the reality of pain and death,
when we hide in the shadows of denial.
Kyrie, eleison.
Walk with us through the valley
of the shadow of death, merciful God,
that we may find the courage to face evil,
knowing that you are on this road with us.
(A time of silence or chanting the Kyrie repetitively may follow.)

Words of Assurance (Isaiah 53, Psalm 22, Hebrews 10)
Bearing the sins of many,
Christ remembers our sins no more.
Offering forgiveness abundantly and lovingly,
Christ gives the gift of a clean heart
and a clear conscience.

Receive this forgiveness,
    and trust in the goodness of God.
Receive this forgiveness,
    and trust in the goodness of God.

Song of Assurance
"What Wondrous Love Is This"

Introduction to the Word (Hebrews 10)
Through Christ, God's covenant of steadfast faith is written in our minds. Through Christ, God's law of love is etched upon our hearts. Let us hold fast to this truth as we listen to the painful story of Jesus' death.

Scripture Reading
John 18:28-38a

Song of Reflection
"Jesus Walked This Lonesome Valley"

—OR—

Song of Reflection
"Ah, Holy Jesus"

Scripture Reading
John 18:38b-19:16a

Song of Reflection
"Beneath the Cross of Jesus"

Scripture Reading
John 19:16b-25a

Song of Reflection
"O Sacred Head, Now Wounded"

Scripture Reading
John 19:25b-37

Song of Remembrance
"O Love Divine, What Hast Thou Done"

Response to the Word (Psalm 22, John 19)
My God, why are so many forsaken?
    Why was Christ betrayed, denied,
    and forsaken?

My God, we cry out, but seldom hear your answer.
Why are we so alone?
In you, we place our trust, and yet we doubt.
In you, we find our life,
and yet, we must also face our death.
My God, why is this day called "Good"?
For all seems forsaken in death.

Scripture Reading
John 19:38-42

Song of Remembrance
"Were You There"

SENDING FORTH

Benediction (Based on the Hymn, "Go to Dark Gethsemane" by James Montgomery)
Go to dark Gethsemane,
    and watch with Christ
    through this time of darkness and sorrow.
Do not turn away from this time of grief,
    but in all things turn to God with prayer.
See Jesus: beaten, bound, reviled, accused,
    condemned, and crucified.
Do not shun suffering or sacrifice,
    but trust that God is with us
    in all of life's suffering.
Walk through the valley of the shadow of death,
    knowing that we do not walk it alone,
    for Christ has walked this lonesome valley,
    and is with us every step of the way.

Optional Song of Sending Forth
"Beneath the Cross of Jesus"

CONTEMPORARY OPTIONS

Contemporary Gathering Words
Come into God's presence,
even when God seems far away.

We cry out and yearn for God.
Listen to the story of Jesus' death,
the saddest story you'll ever hear.
We cry out and yearn for God.
Come into God's presence,
even when God seems far away.

MARCH 31, 2013

Easter Sunday
B. J. Beu

COLOR
White

SCRIPTURE READINGS
Acts 10:34-43; Psalm 118:1-2, 14-24; 1 Corinthians 15:19-26; John 20:1-18 (or Luke 24:1-12)

THEME IDEAS
The steadfast love spoken of by the psalmist has raised Jesus from the dead. How will we recognize our risen savior? Jesus calls each of us by name—a call to discipleship and service. The hymn, "Christ the Lord Is Risen Today" says it all. Everything else is commentary. Yet, before we give ourselves over to Easter celebration, our service can reflect the hopelessness and defeat that Mary and the disciples felt as they came to the tomb. Beginning the service in near darkness with the cross still shrouded with the black cloth of Good Friday is an effective way to capture the surprising truth that death does not have the final word.

INVITATION AND GATHERING
Call to Worship (John 20)
(Begin the service in near darkness, with only an unlit Pascal Candle and a cross shrouded in black cloth on the altar/Lord's

Table. Have a lit votive and small taper hidden behind the Pascal Candle. Place a couple of Easter lilies or other flowers hidden from sight behind the altar/Lord's Table. As the responsive liturgy is read, have a lone liturgical dancer (Mary) approach the chancel with head bowed, carrying a jar symbolizing the anointing oils Mary would have brought to the tomb. As the reading begins, the pianist plays a somber, reflective melody.)

The night is far gone.
There is dew on the grass.
We walk with Mary to the tomb.

(As the reading continues, have one or more angels dressed in billowing white garb come from the side and dance around Mary. Mary continues to grieve as if she cannot perceive them.)

Lost in our grief, we feel abandoned . . . alone . . .
unaware that angels minister to us.

(Pause and let the dancers continue to the tomb, which could be a simulated cave or large stone made out of paper mache.)

We weep with Mary,
for all hope seems lost.
The stone is rolled back.
Only his grave clothes remain.
Overcome by our loss, we feel abandoned . . . alone . . .
unaware that Angels minister to us.

(Change in the music to a more hopeful mood. Mary begins to move with cautious hope.)

A flicker of hope ignites in the soul . . .
wavering in the wind . . .
challenging the triumph of darkness.
Yet, surely there is no cheating death?
Gently, lovingly, angels question our tears . . .
for God is stronger than death.

(One Angel lights the Paschal Candle with the taper hidden behind it while another undrapes the cross. If sanctuary lights are

93

on a dimmer, bring them slowly up to full. The angel who lit the Pascal Candle lifts up an Easter lily or other flower arrangement from behind the altar and places it upon the Lord's Table.)

Out of the shadows of the tomb,
the light of Christ shines forth in glory,
overcoming the darkness of sin and death.
In the depths of our souls,
the light of Christ brings us back
to the land of the living.

(Mary can now see the angels and they all dance together with joy.)

As the light of Christ dawns,
we find that we are not alone.
The light shines in the darkness
and the darkness did not overcome it.

Opening Prayer *(Psalm 118, John 20)*

God of mystery and might,
    your wondrous love
        always seems to catch us off guard.
We come to the tomb
    looking for death,
        but find life instead.
As we behold the glory of our salvation,
    take us back to that moment of discovery—
        when grief and loss gave way
            to a glimmer of hope.
Before we shout our alleluias,
    remind us of the moment
        when despair was transported
            into glimpses of new possibilities.
In the holy awe of Easter morning,
    we take a moment of silent gratitude
        that Christ calls each of us by name.
(Moment of silence.)
Shout it from the mountaintop:

Christ is risen! Alleluia!
Christ is risen indeed.
(The prayer leads naturally into a hymn like "Christ the Lord Is Risen Today.")

Children's Moment
(Before the service, hide the Easter lilies among the pews or choir loft. During the Children's Moment, send the youth on a hunt to find the flowers and then use them to decorate the worship space.)

PROCLAMATION AND RESPONSE

Prayer of Confession (Acts 10)
Resurrected One,
> during your final days,
>> we turned away from you,
>>> even after you shared table with us,
>>>> offering us the bread of heaven
>>>> and the cup of salvation;
>> in your hour of greatest need,
>>> we fell asleep while you prayed in the garden,
>>> even after you urged us to keep the faith
>>>> to avoid the time of trial.

We are here now, dearest friend,
> remembering what it cost you
>> to know the joy we feel today.

May our lives reflect
> the depth of our gratitude
>> to be known as your disciples. Amen.

Words of Assurance (Acts 10, 1 Corinthians 15)
The One who raised Jesus from the dead,
> offers us life and forgiveness of sin.
Rejoice in Christ our savior,
> whose resurrection brings us life.

Response to the Word (Psalm 118)
This is the day that the Lord has made,
> let us rejoice and be glad in it.

For this is the day that Christ rose from the dead,
    bringing life in his name.
In Christ, God has opened the gates of righteousness,
    that those who seek fullness of life
        may enter through it.

THANKSGIVING AND COMMUNION

Offering Prayer (Acts 10)
    God of grace and God of glory,
        pour your power on your people this day,
            that our lives may reflect
                the gift we have received
                    through the resurrection of your Son.
    Truly we see that you show no partiality,
        offering abundance of life and fullness of grace
            to all who turn to you in their need.
    With deepest gratitude for your many gifts,
        particularly the gift of your Son,
            we offer you our tithes and offerings this day.
    In the name of the resurrected one, we pray. Amen.

SENDING FORTH

Benediction (John 20)
    From darkness and despair, we find hope and joy.
        Christ is risen! We go forth in joy!
    From doubt and betrayal, we find trust and faith.
        Christ is risen! We go forth in faith!
    From suffering and death, we find healing and life.
        Christ is risen! We go forth to live!
    Christ is risen. Christ is risen indeed.
        Alleluia.

CONTEMPORARY OPTIONS

Contemporary Gathering Words
    Shout for joy.
        The tomb is empty.

Clap your hands.
Death is cheated.
Dance and sing.
Christ is risen.
Christ is risen.
Christ is risen indeed.

Praise Sentences (Psalm 118, 1 Corinthians 15)

God is stronger than death.
Give thanks to the Lord, for God is good.
Christ is stronger than death!
God's steadfast love endures forever.
The Spirit is stronger than death.
Let everyone shout out:
God's steadfast love endures forever.
Give thanks to the Lord!
God is stronger than death.

APRIL 7, 2013

Second Sunday of Easter

Bill Hoppe

COLOR

White

SCRIPTURE READINGS

Acts 5:27-32; Psalm 150; Revelation 1:4-8; John 20:19-31

THEME IDEAS

God has performed amazing works of immeasurable
greatness, particularly the resurrection of Jesus Christ
from the dead. On this first Sunday after Easter, we share
the conviction of Peter and the apostles who can't help but
share the message of God's love and forgiveness. Yet we
also share the all-too-human doubting of Thomas, as we
struggle to believe the unbelievable. Finally, we join the
psalmist and John by raising our voices in praise and song
for all that God has done for us.

INVITATION AND GATHERING

Call to Worship (Psalm 150)
Praise the Lord!
   Praise God in the sanctuary.
Praise God in the vault of heaven.
   Praise God in the earth and skies.
Sing praises to the Lord.

Shout and sing praises to God.
We have witnessed God's mighty acts.
We have seen the Lord's greatness.
Let everything that breathes praise the Lord.
**Let everything that draws breath
praise the Lord!**

Opening Prayer (Acts 5, John 20)
We hear your calling, Lord;
how can we keep from singing?
How can we keep our lips
from proclaiming the good news,
that Jesus Christ is risen,
bringing healing and forgiveness to all?
From the life in his blood he has freed us,
making us a royal priesthood.
Whether we have seen or believe without seeing,
we have found life in his name.
In Christ's name, we give thanks and praise. Amen!

PROCLAMATION AND RESPONSE

Prayer of Confession (John 20)
Must we see you in order to believe you, Lord?
Is seeing truly believing?
Are we to be prisoners of our senses,
distrusting and rejecting
whatever we cannot see, touch, or hear?
Yet you are faithful—
you give sight to the blind,
you carry us when we are weary,
you call us to your side.
The locked room of our hearts
opens at the turn of your key.
Speak your words of life to us again:
"Do not doubt, only believe."
Speak your words of life,
that we might live.

Words of Assurance (John 20)
The peace of God be with you.
Receive God's forgiveness
   and the promise of the Spirit,
   for Jesus is risen from the dead.
Seen or unseen, he is present in our midst,
   and we see the presence of Christ
   reflected in each other's faces.
Happy are those who have not seen,
   yet have come to believe.

Response to the Word (John 20)
We have listened to your word, Lord.
   **Grant us ears to hear
   what you would have us know.**
We have watched you at work in the world, Lord.
   Grant us eyes to see what you would show us.
You have touched us, Lord.
   **Grant that we may feel your presence,
   and follow your guidance. Amen.**

THANKSGIVING AND COMMUNION

Invitation to the Offering (Psalm 150, John 20, Acts 5, Revelation 1)
What must be done to convince us of God's unending
love? What further proof do we need? We have only to
look around us to see what the Lord has done. We have
only to look to the One who poured out his life for us, who
offered himself in our place, and whose Spirit casts out all
doubt and fear. What can we offer in response? Only our
very selves, and the fruit of our lives and labor.

Offering Prayer (Psalm 150, John 20)
In our songs and in our words,
   we give praise to you, Lord.
In our worship, study, and service,
   we bless you.
Loving God,

you breathe life into our mortal bodies;
 you complete us and fill our every need.
For all that you have done;
 for all that you have given to us,
  we worship you.
Beautiful savior,
  with all that we are, and with all that we have,
  we offer you our thanks and praise. Amen.

SENDING FORTH

Benediction (Acts 5, John 20, Revelation 1)
Peace to you from the One who is and was,
 and is to come.
Grace and peace to you
 from the One who loves us and frees us,
 the One who gives us repentance and forgiveness.
As God sent Jesus into the world,
 so the Spirit now sends us
 to continue God's holy work.
To God be glory and dominion forever and ever!
Amen.

CONTEMPORARY OPTIONS

Contemporary Gathering Words (Acts 5, John 20, Revelation 1)
Jesus Christ: master, leader, savior,
 messiah, faithful witness, Son of God,
 Alpha and Omega, the first and the last,
 the beginning and the end—
  to you be all honor and glory.

Praise Sentences (Acts 5, John 20)
We have seen the Lord! Christ is risen!
There is no fear and no doubt, only belief!
There is life in Jesus' name!

APRIL 14, 2013

Third Sunday of Easter

Sandra Miller

COLOR
White

SCRIPTURE READINGS
Acts 9:1-6 (7-20); Psalm 30; Revelation 5:11-14; John 21:1-19

THEME IDEAS
While this week's scriptures do not expressly say, "Jesus is the light of the world," this is the message conveyed in these passages. Through the risen Christ the veil of our personal egos, our fears, and our sins are all stripped away. Through the risen Christ we are no longer blind. Christ sheds light on the truth of our lives and the source of our salvation.

INVITATION AND GATHERING

Call to Worship (Psalm 30, Revelation 5)
Lord, we come before you in joy,
clothed in the majesty of your glory.
    We come to sing your praises.
Like the myriad faithful of old,
we proclaim the Lamb to be worthy
of blessing, honor, and glory.
    We fall down before you in worship. Amen!

Opening Prayer (Psalm 30)

Compassionate, glorious God,
   you hear our cries,
      and our pleas for help.
We may enter the dark of night with weeping,
   but we wake in the morning with joy,
      for you hear our petitions
         and come in our hour of need.
As we gather here in the name of your Son,
   be with us we pray,
      that we may know the dawn of your mercy,
         and the sweet taste of your favor.

PROCLAMATION AND RESPONSE

Prayer of Confession (Acts 9, Psalm 30)

God of Forgiveness,
   hear now the confession of our sins.
      Our greed and our lust for power
         create enemies where we should find friends.
We fail to offer comfort and aid
   to those who are afraid and beat down
      by the burdens of life.
      We are as blind and willful as Saul
         to the pain and the destruction
            of our wrongdoings
               and our well-meaning crusades.
Forgive us, merciful One.
Give us sight to see with your eyes,
   that we may bring hope peace to our world.
      Amen.

Words of Assurance (Acts 9, Psalm 30)

God's anger lasts but a moment,
   but God's favor lasts a lifetime.
The Lord forgives our shortcomings
   and sends deliverance through Christ,

just as the Lord forgave Saul
and used him to spread the gospel.
Thanks be to God!

Passing the Peace of Christ (Acts 9, Psalm 30)

Christ has taken the scales from our eyes and turned our mourning into dancing. Rejoice with one another, remembering that the peace of Christ is with you.
The peace of Christ is with you always.

Response to the Word (Acts 9, Psalm 30, Revelation 5, John 21)

Great is the glory of God, and great is God's Son
who came to bring salvation to many.
To the one seated on the throne and to the Lamb,
blessing and glory and might forever and ever!
Amen.

THANKSGIVING AND COMMUNION

Invitation to the Offering (John 21)

The holy One has given us fish and bread for a lifetime. Let us now share from our bounty, that through our gifts, God's will may be done.

Offering Prayer (Psalm 30)

Lord, accept these offerings,
given with joy as a token of our praise,
that they may be used in service to Christ.
Thanks be to God.

Invitation to Communion

As we come to the table of God's heavenly feast,
let us prepare our hearts anew
to be in communion with one another
and with the risen Christ.
We come, ready to partake of bread and cup;
ready to commune with one another
and with the living God.

Prayer of Thanksgiving

Gracious God, we give thanks that through Christ,
we live in your favor.
We give thanks that through Christ,
we come to the table of grace
partaking heavenly food
and the gift of salvation.
Like the great company of witnesses
who came to this table before us,
we are filled with gratitude and joy
for your many blessings.
We come before you
in praise and thanksgiving,
as we commit ourselves again
as members of the living body of Christ.

SENDING FORTH

Benediction (Acts 9, Psalm 30)

Go forth from this place with your eyes wide open
as you journey into the wider world.
Love God and see Christ in each person you meet.
Give thanks always
and do not withhold love from any,
for we do not know who may yet turn to the light.

CONTEMPORARY OPTIONS

Contemporary Gathering Words (Psalm 30, Revelation 5, John 21)

Living Creator, the world teems with your beauty
and abounds with your artistry and grace.
We sing your praises, Lord,
as we celebrate the risen Christ.
Celebrate the risen Christ who walks with us
as we traverse the joys and fears of our lives.
We sing your praises, Lord,
as we celebrate the risen Christ.

Praise Sentences (Revelation 5, John 21)

Give boundless thanks to God
    who causes the angels to sing.
Give boundless praise to Christ
    who invites us to follow him.
Give boundless glory to the Spirit
    who makes us one.

APRIL 21, 2013

Fourth Sunday of Easter

Mary J. Scifres

COLOR

White

SCRIPTURE READINGS

Acts 9:36-43; Psalm 23; Revelation 7:9-17; John 10:22-30

THEME IDEAS

God is our Shepherd. Even as the Lamb of God, Christ is our Shepherd (Revelation 7:17). As protector, as guide, as comforter, as savior, as beacon, as the one who calls, Christ is shepherding us through the many hills and valleys of life. In this Easter season, we sing and rejoice with festive music, bright and beautiful sanctuaries, and joy-filled worship services. Yet, even in this festive season, death comes, people wander in dark valleys, and sheep are snatched away from the love that yearns to guide and save them. In the midst of our pain, Christ comes. Whether the hand that lifts us from the darkest valley is that of a fellow traveler or that of a mysterious sense of God alongside, Christ's hand is the hand that reaches to us. Christ's voice is the one that calls to us. Christ's comfort is the one that is offered to us. Revelation reminds us that final judgment can be final blessing; the ones who have endured the greatest ordeals experience the greatest joys, finding the bread that satisfies and the water that quenches every thirst.

INVITATION AND GATHERING

Call to Worship (John 10)
"Come to me," Christ says.
We know and hear this voice.
"Walk with me," Christ calls.
We know and follow this call.
"Live with me," Christ offers.
We rejoice in this promise of life.
Come, let us worship with Easter joy!

Opening Prayer (Psalm 23, Revelation 7)
O Great Shepherd,
    walk with us in this time of worship,
        as you walk with us
            all the days of our lives.
As we sing your praises
    and worship your holy name,
        speak to us with your wisdom,
        call to us and lead us home.
Open our eyes and enlighten our minds,
    that we might hear your word
        and grow in our faith.
In Christ's name, we pray. Amen.

PROCLAMATION AND RESPONSE

Prayer of Confession (Psalm 23, Revelation 7)
Blessing and honor are yours,
    Christ our Lamb and Shepherd.
We sing your praises,
    even as we remember the sorrows and fears
        that haunt our lives.
Wipe away every tear, O God.
Fill every hunger.
Quench every thirst.

Protect us from the sun and sin
   that would burn our souls.
Save us from the dark valleys
   that would lose our paths
     and confuse our journeys.
Lead us beside the healing waters of your grace,
   that we may know the peace of your salvation.

Words of Assurance (Psalm 23)

Surely goodness and mercy shall follow us
   all the days of our lives,
   and we will dwell in the house of God
   forever and ever. Amen.

Passing the Peace of Christ (Psalm 23)

God has restored our souls. Let us restore our relationships with one another as we share signs of love, reconciliation, and peace.

Introduction to the Word (John 10)

Listen for the Shepherd's voice. Listen for the Word of God.

Response to the Word (Psalm 23)

Shepherding God,
   guide us on this journey of life.
Lead us on the paths that lie before us.
Strengthen us in times of fear
   and comfort us in seasons of sorrow.
Renew us in moments of exhaustion,
   that we may lie down to rest in peace.
Surely, your goodness and grace
   are flowing through our lives even now,
   and we rejoice that you dwell with us
     through the power of your Holy Spirit.
In gratitude and joy, we pray. Amen.

THANKSGIVING AND COMMUNION

Invitation to the Offering (Revelation 7)

As we give of ourselves and share God's gifts freely with others, we give blessing and honor to our God. Let us give God glory as we collect this morning's tithes and offerings.

Offering Prayer *(Acts 9, Revelation 7)*

Glory to you, O God,
    for the great things you have done.
For raising us to new life
    as Peter raised Tabitha and Jesus raised Lazarus,
    we are forever grateful.
And so, in gratitude and praise,
    we return these gifts to you,
    that they may be a blessing for others—
        the food of compassion,
            to those who hunger for mercy;
        the water of justice,
            to those who thirst for righteousness;
        the comfort of your love,
            to those who are lost and alone.
In trust and gratitude, we pray. Amen.

Invitation to Communion *(Psalm 23, Revelation 7)*

God has prepared a table where all are welcome: enemies and friends, strangers and neighbors, saints and sinners. The cup of Christ's love overflows with a yearning to fill our lives with abundance. Come, eat of the bread that truly satisfies. Drink of the cup that quenches our thirst for salvation. This is the table of God's love, the feast of Christ's grace. All are welcome here.

SENDING FORTH

Benediction *(Psalm 23, Revelation 7)*

With God as our Shepherd, we go forth.
With Christ as our guide, we go forth.
With God's Spirit showing us the way, we go forth.
With joy and love, we go forth!

CONTEMPORARY OPTIONS

Contemporary Gathering Words *(Psalm 23)*

When we are tired and in need of rest,
shepherd us, O God.

When we are walking in paths of beauty,
shepherd us, O God.
When we are striving to journey in faith,
shepherd us, O God.
When we are frightened and alone,
shepherd us, O God.
When we are angry and feeling threatened,
shepherd us, O God.
When we are hungry and in need of nourishment,
shepherd us, O God.
When we hear your call and turn to follow,
shepherd us, O God.
When we come to worship and praise your name,
shepherd us, O God.

Praise Sentences (Revelation 7)
Blessing and honor are yours!
Glory and power to the Lamb!
Blessing and honor are yours!
Glory and power to the Lamb!

—OR—

Praise Sentences (Revelation 7)
We rejoice with God's saints, today and all days!
We rejoice with God's saints, today and all days!

APRIL 28, 2013

Fifth Sunday of Easter

Mark Sorensen

COLOR

White

SCRIPTURE READINGS

Acts 11:1-18; Psalm 148; Revelation 21:1-6; John 13:31-35

THEME IDEAS

What demands our worship? More significantly, what is truly worthy of our worship? Today's scriptures speak to these questions. They speak of the kind of worship that is big; the kind of worship that is loud; the kind of worship that, when it flows from the heart, spills out into our relationships with everyone we meet. Take a moment and think about this. God dwells among us. Right here, right now. God is with us. Today's scripture call us into the presence of the One who truly is worthy of our praise and adoration.

INVITATION AND GATHERING

Call to Worship (Psalm 148, Revelation 21)
As the sun rises in the morning,
  let all creation worship God!
From the highest mountains to the deepest seas,
  let all creation lift high the name of the Lord,
  for God alone is worthy to be praised.

You alone are worthy of our praise, Alpha and Omega,
Beginning and End.
You alone make all things new.
All praise, glory, and honor be yours, forever.
Amen.

Opening Prayer (Acts 11, Psalm 148)

Gracious and loving God,
    you meet us where we are.
As we gather in this place,
    may our hearts be open to hear your voice,
    may our eyes be open to see your glory,
    and may our minds be open to perceive the word
        you have for each one of us.
We gather together from many walks of life,
    but we are unified as one heart
        in the body of Christ.
Holy Spirit,
    speak to us, guide us, and fall gently upon us,
        we pray. Amen.

PROCLAMATION AND RESPONSE

Prayer of Confession (Psalm 148, John 13)

Eternal God,
    it's so easy to get lost
        in the noise and busyness
            of our lives.
Forgive us the times we lose focus,
    forgetting the praise we owe to you,
    offering it to the world instead.
You alone are worthy of our praise.
You alone are worthy of our adoration.
You alone are worthy of our love.
Creator who makes all things new,
    renew our hearts and strengthen our resolve,
        that we may graciously receive
            what you have in store for us today.

Words of Assurance (Revelation 21)
> When we are thirsty,
>> God renews the soul with living waters.
> Drink deeply, knowing that in Jesus Christ,
>> we are forgiven.

Passing the Peace of Christ (John 13)
> Jesus' command, "Love one another," meets us in this room. Take a moment and turn to your neighbor, sharing the same love God has so richly bestowed upon each of us.

Response to the Word (Acts 11)
> Loving and gracious God,
>> we turn to you in our need.
> Help us be a community
>> that looks to you for guidance.
> Help us be a people
>> that turns to you for the tasks
>>> you would have us do.
> Help us be a church
>> that looks to you for understanding and wisdom,
>>> a church moved by the power and prompting
>>>> of your Holy Spirit in our lives.

THANKSGIVING AND COMMUNION

Offering Prayer (Psalm 148, Revelation 21)
> Holy God,
>> you have given us so much.
> Through your love and abundance,
>> our cup overflows.
> From the bounty of your blessings,
>> we offer these gifts back to you.
> Accept these offerings,
>> that they may be used for your glory,
>>> as we work to bring your kingdom here on earth.
> Amen.

SENDING FORTH

Benediction (John 13)
    As we leave this place,
        may we know that our worship is only beginning;
        may we love others as God has first loved us.
    In all that we see, hear, and take into our hearts,
        may the love of Christ be with us, now and forever.

CONTEMPORARY OPTIONS

Contemporary Gathering Words (Revelation 21)
    Each morning we awake to a blank canvass.
    Our God makes all things new!
    In all circumstances and in all situations,
    Our God makes all things new!
    God is Alpha and Omega, the Beginning and the End.
    Our God makes all things new!

Praise Sentences (Psalm 148)
    Praise the Lord! May God's name be exalted
    and lifted high among the nations!
    **Praise the Lord! May God's name be exalted
    and lifted high among the nations!**

MAY 5, 2013

Sixth Sunday of Easter

B. J. Beu

COLOR

White

SCRIPTURE READINGS

Acts 16:9-15; Psalm 67; Revelation 21:1-10, 22–22:5; John 14:23-29

THEME IDEAS

The Easter season is a time for sheer delight, a time to praise God with renewed faith and vision. The psalmist invites us to praise God for saving us, guiding us, and blessing us. Revelation provides a deeper sense of God's saving power, promising a new heaven and a new earth, where nations will walk in the light of the Lamb. Mourning and weeping will be no more, for God will wipe away every tear. The Gospel eases our sense of loss at Christ's departure, for God has sent us the Advocate, the Holy Spirit, to bring us peace, take away our fear, and lead us into truth. Take delight in God, for we are never alone on our journey of faith.

INVITATION AND GATHERING

Call to Worship (Psalm 67, John 14)
Let the peoples praise you, O God.
Let all the peoples praise you.

Let all nations be glad and sing for joy.
For you judge the peoples with justice and truth.
Let all the ends of the earth revere you, Holy One.
For you bless your people with peace and hope.
Let the peoples praise you, O God.
Let all the peoples praise you!

Opening Prayer (Acts 16, John 14)

Guiding Spirit,
you come to us in visions and dreams,
calling us beyond the narrow confines
of our waking perceptions.
Open our hearts this day,
as you opened the heart of Lydia before us,
that we might understand Christ's teaching,
and share his presence with those we meet.
Guide our footsteps on our journey,
as you guided Paul's footsteps
around the shores of the Mediterranean Sea,
that we may go where you send us
to share your message of love and peace
with a world scarred by hate
and violence. Amen.

PROCLAMATION AND RESPONSE

Prayer of Confession (John 14:27)

God of love,
we have not always kept your word,
nor loved you as we ought.
Trapped in our suffering,
we have withheld forgiveness from others
and locked our hearts away from love.
Send your Advocate to us once more,
that we may feel in our bones
the peace Christ promised his followers:
"Peace I leave with you;
my peace I give to you.

I do not give to you as the world gives.
Do not let your hearts be troubled,
    and do not let them be afraid."
May it be so, O God.
May it be so.

Words of Assurance (Revelation 21–22)
The new heaven and new earth are surely coming,
    when we will drink from the spring
    of the water of life.
The One who is faithful will wipe away every tear
    and make all things new.
Receive forgiveness in the light of the Lamb,
    in whom there is no darkness at all.
Receive forgiveness from the One who brings us peace.

Response to the Word (John 14)
Christ's words are true.
    Teach us, Holy Spirit.
Christ's words bring life.
    Heal us, Holy Spirit.
Christ is speaking still.
    Lead us, Holy Spirit.

THANKSGIVING AND COMMUNION

Invitation to the Offering (Psalm 67, Revelation 21–22)
The One who is our lamp and our light does not leave us
in darkness, but grants us the vision to see the new heaven
and new earth that is within our midst when we live as
God's holy people. As we collect today's offering, may our
gifts help wipe away one another's tears, even as we an-
ticipate the time when God will dwell among us, and
wipe away every tear.

Offering Prayer (Psalm 67, Revelation 21–22)
We praise your name, O God,
    for the bounty of your love.

You cause the earth to yield food
   to satisfy the hungry.
You send rain upon the earth
   to give drink to the thirsty.
You shine light into our darkness
   to show us the way.
Bless these offerings this day,
    that through these gifts,
       the world may touch your love. Amen.

SENDING FORTH

Benediction (Psalm 67, Revelation 21–22, John 14)
   The new heaven and new earth
   are found in Christ's words of peace:
   "Peace I leave with you.
   My peace I give to you."
     In Christ, we find peace.
   The home of God is touched when Christ's words
   flow through our lives like water:
   "I do not give to you as the world gives."
     In Christ, we taste springs of living water.
   God's face shines upon us
   through Christ's message of comfort:
   "Do not let your hearts be troubled,
   and do not let them be afraid."
     In Christ, we lay aside our fear
     and live as God intends.

CONTEMPORARY OPTIONS

Contemporary Gathering Words (Psalm 67)
   Sing and shout for joy.
   God's light shines upon us.
     Sing praises to God, sing praises.
   Sing and shout for joy.
   God's light shines within us.
     Sing praises to God, sing praises.

Sing and shout for joy.
God's light shines through us.
Sing praises to God, sing praises.

Praise Sentences or Benediction (Easter)

Hear the good news: Christ is risen!
Praise the One who conquers death.
Live the good news: Christ is risen!
Praise the One who brings us life.
Share the good news: Christ is risen indeed!
Praise the One who leads us home.

MAY 12, 2013

Seventh Sunday of Easter / Festival of the Christian Home / Mother's Day

Mary J. Scifres

COLOR

White

SCRIPTURE READINGS

Acts 16:16-34; Psalm 97; Revelation 22:12-14, 16-17, 20-21; John 17:20-26

THEME IDEAS

This Seventh Sunday of Easter may also be celebrated as Ascension Sunday, using lections from Acts 1:1-11; Psalm 47; Ephesians 1:15-23; and Luke 24:44-53. Whichever scriptures are used, this is a day that shows God's power to the world. Jesus calls the disciples to be one, not only with each other, but also with him. Through this unity of spirit, the world may know God's presence through the disciples' ministry. In Acts, Paul has the power to heal a girl suffering from demon possession—a healing that leads to transformation throughout the town as people witness this miraculous act. The glory of God is proclaimed in both Psalm 97 and Revelation 22. God's glory is evident even to the heavens, so that the world may know God. This is the ministry to which the disciples will

soon be sent—the ministry of showing and proclaiming
God's glorious presence to the world.

INVITATION AND GATHERING

Call to Worship (Revelation 22)
"Come," says the Spirit. "Come."
"Come," say the people. "Come."
Let everyone who is thirsty come.
All who yearn for the water of life are welcome.
"Come," says Christ, our Alpha and Omega. "Come."
"Come," say our sisters and brothers. "Come."
Come! Let us worship God together.

Opening Prayer (Revelation 22, John 17)
Glorious, amazing God,
　　as we begin this time of worship,
　　　　we remember that you are both our beginning
　　　　　　and our end.
There is nothing in the world
　　that was not created by you—
　　　　even we are the works of your hands.
There is nothing more glorious in the world
　　than your love and grace—
　　　　even we abide in your love and grace.
Be with us now,
　　as you have been with us
　　　　every moment of our lives.
Help us know that we are one with you,
　　one with each other,
　　　　and one in ministry to the world.
In your holy name, O Alpha and Omega,
　　we pray. Amen.

PROCLAMATION AND RESPONSE

Prayer of Confession (Acts 16, Psalm 97, Revelation 22)
God of grace and glory,
　　shine in our lives,

that we may shine in the lives of others.
Strengthen us with the courage of Paul,
that we may heal those
who are crying out to you.
Guard our lives,
that we may be faithful
in all that we say and do.
Dawn upon us with wisdom and truth,
that we may be instruments of grace and love,
proclaiming your glory through our lives.

Words of Assurance (Psalm 97)

God guards the lives of the faithful,
rescuing them from the hands of the wicked.
Light has dawned.
Joy and forgiveness are ours
through the grace of Jesus Christ.

Passing the Peace of Christ (John 17)

Christ prayed that we might be one, as Jesus and God, our
heavenly Mother and Father, are one. Let us share signs of
unity and love, as we pass the peace that is ours through
Christ Jesus, who lives in us and in this community of
faith.

Response to the Word

(Hand strips of construction paper to participants as they enter
worship. Provide pencils or crayons throughout the seating area.
During the sermon or immediately following, invite worshipers
to jot down a word or draw a picture of difficulties or "demons"
that are haunting their lives. After the message time, or during
the collection of the morning offering, provide the means for
people to staple their strips into linked circles to form chains.
Place the chains together in the front of the sanctuary. Following the collection of "chain links," offer this or a similar prayer.)
God of earthquake and lightning,
strike down the chains that bind us.
Release us from the difficulties that enslave us.
Help us spring forth with new life and hope

as we shine with your glory.
Guide us in your freedom and grace,
    that our lives may reflect your righteousness.

THANKSGIVING AND COMMUNION

Offering Prayer (Psalm 97)

Gracious, glorious God,
    you have given us so much
        for which we are ever grateful.
As we return these gifts to you,
    bless them with your presence.
Glorify the works of these gifts in the world,
    that your love and salvation
        may shine through them for all to see.

Prayers of the People (John 17, Mother's Day)

God of mothers and fathers,
    young and old, friends and neighbors,
        be present in the needs of our world.
As we gather on this day of celebration and praise,
    we are thankful for the many people who mother us
        and nurture us to grow in faith and wisdom.
Be with those who are mothers for others.
Strengthen them with your grace and knowledge.
We pray for mothers and fathers around the world,
    especially for those who are struggling
        to find food and security for their children.
We pray for children and youth throughout the world,
    especially for those who are in need
        of mothers and mentors in their lives.
For those who mourn this day, give comfort.
For those who yearn this day, give patience.
For those who are torn apart by grief and resentment,
    may your healing love bring forgiveness
        and reconciliation.
Let all who hunger and thirst for your presence
    know the living water that is ours without limit

through Christ Jesus.
In his holy name, we pray. Amen.

Communion Prayer (John 17)
Mother Father God,
pour out your Spirit and Power
upon these gifts of bread and wine.
Make them be for us your loving presence,
living in us and through us.
As your Spirit calls us to unity,
through the power of Christ Jesus,
make us one with you, one with each other,
and one in ministry to the world.

SENDING FORTH

Benediction (Revelation 22, John 17)
May the grace of the Lord Jesus be with you
as you go forth, empowered and strengthened,
to love and serve as Christ leads.

CONTEMPORARY OPTIONS

Contemporary Gathering Words (Revelation 22)
Come, you who are thirsty for love and grace.
The water of life is God's gift.
Come, you who are thirsty for justice and peace.
The water of life is God's gift.
Come, you who are thirsty for God.
The water of life is God's gift.
Come, the water is God's gift,
flowing freely as we worship together.
The water of life is God's gift!

Praise Sentences (Psalm 97)
God is King! Let the earth rejoice!
God is King! Let the earth rejoice!

MAY 19, 2013

Pentecost Sunday
Mary Petrina Boyd

COLOR
Red

SCRIPTURE READINGS
Acts 2:1-21; Psalm 104:24-34, 35b; Romans 8:14-17; John 14:8-17 (25-27)

THEME IDEAS
Acts 2:1-21 is the central scripture for Pentecost Sunday, telling how the Holy Spirit descended upon the disciples, empowering them to witness to the gospel before all people. Psalm 104 reminds us that God's Spirit has been present from the beginning, creating and renewing all that is. Romans tells us that through God's Spirit, we are adopted as God's children and are heirs with Christ. In John, Jesus reassures the disciples that God will send the Spirit of truth to teach and remind them of all he has told them. Through these texts, we encounter God's Spirit—the Spirit that creates, renews, empowers, teaches, and draws us into a deeper relationship with God and with one another.

INVITATION AND GATHERING

Call to Worship (Acts 2)
First we hear the sound . . .
like the rush of a violent wind.

Then we see tongues of fire...
resting upon each person.
Then we feel the Spirit...
giving us words to speak.
The Spirit blesses all...
young and old, women and men.
Come Holy Spirit...
renew us this day and make us your own.

Opening Prayer (Acts 2, Psalm 104, Romans 8)
Come Spirit,
blow through our lives
with the power of your love.
Create us anew
with the winds of your grace.
May the fires of your hope
burn away our fears.
May the power of your compassion
remake us into a Pentecost people.
Gather us up,
fill us with good things,
and teach us to speak with wisdom and power.
Amen.

PROCLAMATION AND RESPONSE

Prayer of Confession (Acts 2, John 14)
Spirit of power and grace,
confused and bewildered by your power,
we turn aside from your transforming grace;
uncertain about the future,
we allow our troubles and fears
to keep us from tasting your promised joy.
We fail to welcome the grace
of your healing love into our hearts.
We want proof before we are satisfied.
Give us trusting hearts,
that we may hear your word,

welcome your spirit,
>> and proclaim your love to all the world. Amen.

Words of Assurance (Acts 2, Romans 8)
God pours out a spirit of love and power on all people,
>> recreating us into powerful witnesses
>> as children of God.

Passing the Peace of Christ (John 14)
Jesus said to his disciples, "Peace I leave you; my peace I
give to you." Receive the gift of Christ's peace and share
that gift with one another.

Prayer of Preparation (Acts 2)
On Pentecost, all in Jerusalem heard your word
>> in their native tongues.
Send the power of the Spirit upon us now,
>> that we may hear your words spoken for us today,
>> in our own language, in our own time.

Response to the Word (Acts 2)
Spirit of God,
>> recreate, renew, and restore us this day.
Open us to the power of your transforming Spirit,
>> that we may proclaim your love,
>> make known your gifts,
>> and share your blessing with all of the world. Amen.

THANKSGIVING AND COMMUNION

Offering Prayer (Acts 2, Psalm 104)
By your love, holy God,
>> you have created all that is.
In your Spirit you renew creation.
Use our gifts to help bring justice and mercy
>> to those in need.
Send your Spirit upon us and transform us,
>> that our world might know your love.
We offer our gifts,
>> **knowing that they come from your Spirit.**

We offer our lives,
trusting that your Spirit will transform us.

Great Thanksgiving (Acts 2, Psalm 104, John 14, Luke 14:18-19)

The Lord be with you.
And also with you
Open your hearts.
We open our hearts to God's Spirit.
Let us praise the God who creates!
Let us praise the God who renews!

God of fire and wind,
we praise you for your continuing work
of creation, renewal, and blessing.
In the beginning of time,
as you called the world into being,
you sent the breath of your spirit
across the formless void and darkness,
calling creation into being.
To your servants, you sent gifts of your Spirit:
to Moses, a spirit of courage,
to Joshua, a spirit of wisdom,
to David, a spirit of power.
You sent your Spirit upon your prophet Isaiah,
who prophesied that you would call forth a leader
with a spirit of wisdom and understanding,
a spirit of counsel and might,
a spirit of knowledge and reverence.
You sent your Spirit upon your prophet Joel,
who proclaimed that you would send your Spirit
upon all people: young and old, women and men.

With all those Spirit-filled people,
we join in singing God's praise:
**Holy, holy, holy Lord, God of power and might,
heaven and earth are full of your glory.**

**Hosanna in the highest. Blessed is the one
who comes in the name of the Lord.
Hosanna in the highest.**

In the fullness of time,
  your Holy Spirit entered the life of Mary,
  who gave birth to your Son, Jesus.
As Jesus began his ministry, he proclaimed:
  "The Spirit of the Lord is upon me,
  to bring good news to the poor.
  to proclaim release to the captives
  and recovery of sight to the blind,
  to let the oppressed go free,
  to proclaim the year of the Lord's favor."
As he prepared his disciples for their ministry,
  Jesus promised to send the Spirit of truth—
  to abide with them, to teach them,
  and to remind them of his words.
In his living, in his loving, and in his teaching,
  Jesus challenged the powers of the world.

On the night he was betrayed,
  Jesus gathered at table with his friends.
He took bread, offered thanks, broke the bread
  and shared it with them, saying:
  "This is myself, a gift for you.
  As you eat this bread, remember me."
After the meal, Jesus took the cup
  and shared it with them, saying,
  "This is the power of my life,
  offered as a new covenant of forgiveness.
  As you drink this cup, remember me."

In remembering we become the body of Christ.
And so with all creation,
we proclaim the mysteries of faith:
  Christ has died.

Christ is risen.
Christ will come again.

Spirit of power, as the flames of grace
   descended upon the followers of Jesus,
   send the power of your Spirit
      upon all of us gathered here.
Give us courage, give us wisdom,
   give us words, give us power,
      that we may be the body of Christ,
         carrying your message of grace
            to all the world.
Transforming Spirit of love,
   rest upon these gifts of bread and cup,
   that they may be the gift of Christ's presence—
      feeding us, renewing our hope,
         transforming our fears, blessing our lives.
Through your child, Jesus Christ,
   with the Holy Spirit, the Advocate,
   we sing your praises, Almighty God,
      now and forevermore.
Amen.

SENDING FORTH

Benediction (Acts 2, John 14)
   Go into the world, proclaiming God's power.
   Carry the Spirit of truth to places of pain and struggle.
   Carry the Spirit of peace to places of fear and despair.
   May that peace dwell within your hearts.

—OR—

Benediction (John 14)
   Jesus gave us peace.
   It is a true gift from the one whose name is love.
   Do not let your hearts be troubled.
   Do not let them be afraid.
   Live in the peace that Jesus gives.

—OR—

Benediction (John 14)

Jesus said, "Peace I leave with you.
"My peace I give to you.
"Do not let your hearts be troubled.
"Do not let them be afraid."
Go in peace this day.
Go with the Spirit's blessing.

CONTEMPORARY OPTIONS

Contemporary Gathering Words (Acts 2)

God says, "I will pour out my Spirit."
What does this mean?
God says, "I will pour out my Spirit on all people."
Who will receive God's Spirit?
Old and young, men and women, people of all kinds.
What will God's Spirit bring?
Visions for truth, dreams of peace.
Come Holy Spirit, come!
Fill our hearts with your love.
Bless us with your Spirit!

Praise Sentences (Acts 2, Romans 8, Psalm 104, John 14)

We are God's children! We are adopted by God's love!
Sing to the Lord. Rejoice with God.
Bless the Lord, O my soul. Praise the Lord!
The Spirit of God rests upon us.
The Spirit of God hovers over us.
The Spirit of God burns away our fears.
The Spirit of God brings peace.
Thanks be to God!

MAY 26, 2013

Trinity Sunday
Jamie D. Greening

COLOR
White

SCRIPTURE READINGS
Proverbs 8:1-4, 22-31; Psalm 8; Romans 5:1-5;
John 16:12-15

THEME IDEAS
In Proverbs, Wisdom calls out like a wise woman, warning and encouraging us at the crossroads of life. In Psalm
8, the call is about the nature of creation, while in Romans
5, the Lord calls out to us about faith, grace, and salvation
in Christ. In John 16, the Holy Spirit beckons us into the
path of truth. Wisdom is spiritual enlightenment, and in
each of these readings, we find that she is calling us to a
deeper understanding of and relationship with God.

INVITATION AND GATHERING

Call to Worship (Proverbs 8, Romans 5, John 16)
To you, O people, Wisdom calls.
She calls out to each of us, beckoning us:
    to experience peace in Christ,
    to discover the truth of life,
    to know true love as it is poured into our hearts.

Wisdom calls.
As we gather this day,
   let us answer her call
   as we celebrate faith
   in the One who leads us into life.
(alternate ending)
   in Jesus Christ as Lord.

—OR—

Call to Worship (Psalm 8)
*(The attributes of God are said by eight different people, scat-
tered throughout the worship space. The last phrase is said by
the worship leader.)*
O Lord, our Sovereign,
   your name is:
      Majestic,
      Compassionate,
      Glorious,
      Inspiring,
      Beautiful,
      Amazing,
      Tender,
      Powerful.
All-encompassing Lord,
   your name is blessed in all the earth.

Opening Prayer (Proverbs 8, Psalm 8)
O Lord,
   you reveal wisdom and spiritual insight
      through your presence in creation.
When we look at the heavens,
   we see your vastness.
When we look at seas teeming with fish
   and verdant fields painted like a canvas,
      we see your creativity and your bounty.
For all of this and so much more,
   we praise your name. Amen.

—*OR*—

Opening Prayer (Romans 5, John 16)

We thank you, O Lord,
>that you give us love and peace
>>through Christ Jesus;
>that you offer us the key to all spiritual knowledge
>>through your Holy Spirit.

For those who are in the midst of life's problems,
>grant your wisdom and insight from above.

For those who are burdened with anxiety and fear,
>offer your wise assurance in times of need.

For those facing decisions about family or career,
>bless them with your wisdom on high.

For those entering a new chapter in their lives,
>be it the birth of children, taking new jobs,
>finding a place to live, or entering retirement,
>>guide them on the proper path
>>>and bless them with a sense of peace.

This we pray in the name and wisdom
>of Jesus Christ our Lord. Amen.

PROCLAMATION AND RESPONSE

Prayer of Confession (Proverbs 8, Psalm 8, Romans 5, John 16)

God of infinite mercy,
>when we neglect the humbleness
>>of knowing our place in this world,
>>>forgive us;
>when we trade your peace and calls for unity
>>for conflict and violence,
>>>forgive us;
>when we forsake our good character,
>>to join those who scoff at your ways,
>>>forgive us;
>when we ignore your truth,
>>and turn away from your wisdom,
>>>forgive us.

Forgive us and heal us, Lord,
    that we may abide in your grace
      and your love forever. Amen.

Words of Assurance (Romans 5)
Through the power of the Holy Spirit,
    God fills our souls with grace and wisdom.
It is from this grace that we have hope.
It is from this wisdom that we know God's love.
It is from the living God
    that we find life and forgiveness.

Passing the Peace (Romans 5)
Since we have peace with God through Jesus Christ, let
us stand and share this peace with one another.

Prayer of Preparation (Proverbs 8, Psalm 8, Romans 5, John 16)
Teach us your wisdom, O Lord,
    that we may live wisely, not foolishly.
Open our minds to understand our place in the world,
    that we may be proper stewards and caretakers
      of this beautiful earth.
May your love and wisdom flow through us,
    into this world of hatred and mistrust,
      that we may sow the seeds of peace.
Illumine our hearts to the path of truth, Holy Spirit,
    that we may celebrate the ways that lead to life. Amen.

Response to the Word (Proverbs 8)
The word of the Lord is wisdom
May we live as a people both good and wise.

THANKSGIVING AND COMMMUNION

Invitation to the Offering (Proverbs 8, Psalm 8)
Through holy wisdom, the Lord has made the world as a
rich dwelling place, giving us dominion over the created
order. As God is mindful of us and of our needs, let us
now be mindful of our obligation to be good stewards,
through our generosity and responsibility for God's gifts.

Offering Prayer (Proverbs 8, Psalm 8)

O Lord,
   we rejoice with thankful hearts,
      that you have given us this beautiful world
         in which to work and play—
            a world full of your wisdom
               and majesty;
      we offer praise with deepest gratitude,
         that you have blessed us with your bounty.
As we return a portion of your blessing to us,
   use these offerings and tokens of our devotion:
      to increase wisdom in the world,
      to protect the created order,
      to bless the vulnerable,
      to heal the sick,
         and to comfort the afflicted. Amen.

Invitation to Communion (Proverbs 8, Psalm 8, Romans 5, John 16)

(Consider using as a call and response between two readers)
Wisdom calls:
   Come eat the bread of life.
Wisdom calls:
   Come drink the cup of fellowship.
Wisdom calls:
   Come partake of truth and grace.
Wisdom calls:
   Come and be enlightened by the Holy Spirit.

Communion Prayer (Proverbs 8, Psalm 8, Romans 5, John 16)

Almighty, majestic, and sovereign Lord,
   our hearts are stirred by the power of your wisdom.
In the very elements of creation,
   you have displayed your power and might
      for every soul to perceive.
And yet, a deeper wisdom is revealed
   in the bread and the cup.
We celebrate today that this wisdom is gained by faith,
   and it is through grace that we may partake.

As we partake of these simple yet profound elements,
    whisper into our hearts,
        and speak the truth we long to hear.
Holy Spirit, guide us into truth about ourselves,
    our world, our church, and your ways,
        that we may be transformed.
Open our eyes to deep spiritual wisdom,
    as we participate in the ancient work
        of Holy Communion.

SENDING FORTH

Benediction (Proverbs 8, Romans 5)
Through grace and peace,
may we have the wisdom to be transformed.
    For suffering leads to endurance,
    endurance gives rise to character,
    and character produces hope.
In true hope, hope founded in God,
we are never disappointed.

CONTEMPORARY OPTIONS

Contemporary Gathering Words (Proverbs 8, Psalm 8, Romans 5)
I hear a noise. I hear a sound. Do you hear it?
    It is Wisdom calling.
Where is she? Where can I find her?
    She calls from the heights of the heavens
    and speaks with truth on her lips.
May I come? May I learn?
    Yes, you may come. You may learn.
    Wisdom calls all people
    to faith, peace, love, and hope.

Praise Sentences (Proverbs 8, Psalm 8, Romans 5, John 15)
Our Sovereign Lord is majestic,
    filling our hearts with song.
Our Sovereign Lord is wise,

ennobling our minds with truth.
Our Sovereign Lord is gracious,
    empowering our souls with strength.
Our Sovereign Lord is loving,
    blessing us with peace.

JUNE 2, 2013

Second Sunday after Pentecost
Mary J. Scifres

COLOR
Green

SCRIPTURE READINGS
1 Kings 18:20-39; Psalm 96; Galatians 1:1-12; Luke 7:1-10

THEME IDEAS
Even those who profess God with their lips often reject God's gifts and grace through their actions. The Israelites fell into idolatrous worship of Baal. The Galatians were confused by new teachings that rejected the grace and guidance of Christ. The scribes and Pharisees rejected Jesus, even as a centurion turned to him for a healing miracle. Who is this Jesus who would heal the slave of a Roman leader? Who is this God who would send down fire to show even the prophets of Baal that Yahweh is God of all creation, Savior of all the nations, Lover of all peoples? This is our God. This is the God we worship. This is the God we serve. But the gifts and grace of God are not for us alone, they are for all of God's creation and all of the earth's peoples.

INVITATION AND GATHERING
Call to Worship (Psalm 96) ¹¹\5\20
Sing a new song of gratitude and praise!
Our God is God of all creation!

Great is the Lord, and great is God's love.
God's love calls us here.
Let the heavens be glad. Let the mountains rejoice.
Even the trees sing for joy,
for God is God of all!

Opening Prayer (1 Kings 18, Psalm 96)

God of heaven and earth,
    we call upon your name
        as we gather for worship and praise.
Hear our prayers,
    and heed our cries,
        as we yearn to grow closer to you.
Shower us with your grace,
    and light the fire of wisdom in our minds.
Bless us with your presence,
    that we may walk in your truth,
        and live in your righteousness,
        all the days of our lives. Amen.

PROCLAMATION AND RESPONSE

Prayer of Confession (1 Kings 18, Psalm 96)

God of grace and glory,
    you know our times of weakness—
        when we have not reflected your glory,
        when we have rejected your grace,
        when we have doubted your presence
            in our lives.
Speak to us now.
Hear our cries of remorse
    for our moments of darkness, fear, and neglect.
Shine upon us with the light of your mercy,
    that we may see your presence ever more clearly
    and know your grace ever more intimately.
Shine radiantly through us,
    that we may glorify you.
Shine bright within us,

that we may reflect the glory of your love
 flowing through our lives.
In Christ's name, we pray. Amen.

Words of Assurance (Psalm 96, Galatians 1)

Sing for joy with all the earth,
 for Christ is coming, and is with us even now.
In Christ, we are shown grace upon grace;
 we are offered forgiveness and reconciliation,
 that we may once again be united with God,
 as Christ's holy people.

Passing the Peace of Christ (Galatians 1, Colossians 3)

As Christ's holy people, beloved and chosen, we are given
grace upon grace. Let us share signs of grace and peace
with one another in remembrance of this miraculous gift
of God.

Prayer of Preparation (1 Kings 18)

Holy, holy, holy Lord,
 speak to our hearts.
Rain down upon our spirits,
 with your fiery Spirit
 of wisdom and understanding.
Send your word to us, we pray,
 that we might hear
 and know that you are God.
Holy, holy, holy Lord,
 speak to our hearts this day. Amen.

Response to the Word (1 Kings 18, Psalm 96, Isaiah 40, John 1)

Have you not known? Have you not heard?
 The Lord is God,
 full of glory and grace.
If the Lord is God, will you not follow;
will you not live in this truth?
 Our God is an awesome God,
 full of mercy and love.

Follow as children of mercy, as givers of love.
We will follow as disciples of Christ.

THANKSGIVING AND COMMUNION

Offering Prayer (1 Kings 18)
Bless these offerings
    we return to you, O God.
Rain upon them with the holy fire
    of your miraculous grace and love,
      that as these gifts go forth into the world,
        people may sense your presence
          and know your power and love.
In your holy name, we pray. Amen.

Invitation to Communion (1 Kings 18)
Come closer to God.
Come to the Holy of Holies.
Come into the presence of the One who created us
    and claims us as children of love.
Come closer, for all are welcome here.

The Great Thanksgiving (1 Kings 18, Isaiah 40)
The Lord be with you.
    And also with you.
Lift up your hearts.
    We lift them up to the Lord.
Let us give thanks to the Lord, our God.
    It is right to give our thanks and praise.

It is right, and a good and joyful thing,
    always and everywhere to give you thanks,
    Almighty God, creator of heaven and earth.
From everlasting to everlasting,
    you have revealed your mighty presence to us.
Have we not heard? Have we not known?
In the beginning, you swept across the earth
    with your Spirit of life and renewal.
When we forgot or neglected your truth,

you redeemed us and renewed us.
From the earth's first gardens to mountaintop storms,
 you have spoken to us,
 and entrusted us to be your people.
From laws on tablets to warnings from prophets,
 you have spoken your truth
 and renewed your covenant with us,
 reviving us and reclaiming us
 through your grace and love.

And so, with your people on earth,
 with all of creation,
 and with all the company of heaven,
 we sing this ancient song, ever new,
 as we praise your name
 and join their unending hymn, saying:
 Holy, holy, holy Lord, God of power and might,
 heaven and earth are full of your glory.
 Hosanna in the highest. Blessed is the one
 who comes in the name of the Lord.
 Hosanna in the highest.

Holy are you and blessed is your holy name.
In the fullness of time, you sent your Son, Jesus Christ
 to reveal your powerful love for the world.
Healing and teaching, proclaiming and prophesying,
 welcoming any and all,
 Christ continues to reveal your presence,
 renewing our souls even now.
Through Christ's powerful love and endless grace,
 we are invited into your presence,
 rescued from our sins, and led onto your path
 of justice and righteousness.
In Christ's grace, you renew and reclaim us
 as your holy people, children of mercy and truth.
As children of your covenant of love,
 sealed by water and the Spirit,

we come to you now with joy and gratitude,
remembering how Jesus shared bread and wine,
renewing and reviving the lives of
his closest friends, his most faithful disciples,
even as they faced their deepest fears
and their greatest sins.

On that night before his death, Jesus took bread,
gave thanks to you, broke the bread,
gave it to his disciples, and said,
"Take, eat; this is my body which is given for you.
Do this in remembrance of me."
When the supper was over, Jesus took the cup,
gave thanks to you, gave it to his disciples,
and said, "Drink from this, all of you;
this is my life in the new covenant,
poured out for you and for many
for the forgiveness of sins.
Do this, as often as you drink it,
in remembrance of me."

And so, in remembrance of these
your life-giving acts of love and grace,
we offer ourselves in praise and thanksgiving,
as children of your covenant,
renewed and redeemed by your grace,
in union with Christ's love for us,
as we proclaim the mystery of faith.
Christ has died.
Christ is risen.
Christ will come again.

Communion Prayer

Pour out the fire of your Holy Spirit
on all of us gathered here
and on these gifts of bread and wine.
Make them be for us the life and love of Christ,
that we may be for the world

your community of love and justice,
    redeemed by Christ's mercy and grace.
In your Spirit, claim us as your own,
    make us one with Christ,
        one with each other,
            and one in ministry to all the world,
                until Christ comes in final victory
                    and we feast at the heavenly banquet.
Through Jesus Christ,
    with the Holy Spirit in your holy Church,
        all honor and glory is yours, Almighty God,
            now and forever more.
    Amen.

Giving the Bread and Cup
(The bread and wine are given to the people, with these or other words of blessing.)
The life of Christ, living in you.
The love of Christ, flowing through you.

SENDING FORTH

Benediction (1 Kings 18, Psalm 96, Luke 7)
Go forth with songs of joy.
Go forth with stories of hope.
Go forth with faith in the miracle of love.
Go forth as the children of God.

CONTEMPORARY OPTIONS

Contemporary Gathering Words (1 Kings 18, Psalm 96, Luke 7)
Wet wood that bursts into flames...
Trees that break forth into song...
Roman slaves that are healed at the brink of death...
These are the stories of our faith:
    legends of old, God's promises ever new.
Enter into the story, for this is your story:
    Lives dampened by despair

bursting with the joy of new hope...
Souls shrouded in silence
    suddenly singing of God's glory and love...
Strangers and sinners
    welcomed into Christ's promise
    of life everlasting...
These are the stories of our faith:
    legends of this very day, God's promises ever new.

Praise Sentences (Psalm 96)

Sing a new song of hope!
Sing a new song of hope!
Rejoice with the heavens and earth!
Rejoice with the heavens and earth!

JUNE 9, 2013

Third Sunday after Pentecost
Hans Holznagel

COLOR
Green

SCRIPTURE READINGS
1 Kings 17:8-24; Psalm 146; Galatians 1:11-24; Luke 7:11-17

THEME IDEAS
In all her well-known social and economic vulnerability in the ancient Middle East, few biblical characters embody the poor and oppressed more fully than the widow. In today's stories, it is clear that the widows of the world are precisely whom God cares about. Elijah is sent by the Lord to a widow (I Kings 17); Jesus is moved by a widow's plight (Luke 7). Both of these prophets of God become agents of miracles, showing holy love for those who have no refuge in society (Psalm 146).

INVITATION AND GATHERING

Call to Worship (Psalm 146)
Praise the Lord.
    Let all who draw breath praise the Lord.
Happy are those whose help is from God—
the One who made heaven and earth,
the One who created the seas and all that is in them.

Happy are those whose hope is in God—
the One who keeps faith forever,
the One who feeds the hungry
and defends the oppressed.
God will reign forever, for all generations.
Praise the Lord!
Let all who draw breath praise the Lord.

Opening Prayer (Psalm 146)

O God, who lifts us up,
sets us free, and watches over us,
visit us this day.
Lift our spirits,
and free our minds.
Open our eyes and hearts
to your words, your will,
and the miracle of your holy presence,
that we may encounter you
in the meeting of friends
and in kindness to strangers.
Lift us up, and set us free, O God.
Watch over us, we pray. Amen.

PROCLAMATION AND RESPONSE

Prayer of Confession (Psalm 146, 1 Kings 17)

Merciful God,
you know how we love miracles.
We love your healing, life-giving presence.
We confess that poverty and oppression
are less appealing topics.
Yet, we find you among the poor,
the downtrodden, the widow, the orphan.
In their midst we find you,
your prophets, and your miracles.
Dwell with us,
as we make the struggles of the oppressed
our own struggles.

Join us at your table,
    as we join the effort to feed and clothe
        those who live in want.
Grant us your compassion, we pray,
    that we may truly be your people. Amen.

Words of Assurance (Psalm 146, Luke 7)

Hear the good news:
    Those who seek will find help and hope in God.
In Jesus we are raised to newness of life.
Thanks be to God.

Passing the Peace of Christ (Luke 7)

As Jesus drew crowds in Galilee, so he draws us here today. We are not alone. Let us greet one another with signs of God's peace.
The peace of Christ be with you.
And also with you.

Response to the Word (1 Kings 17)

Feed us, O God,
    from stores that never empty.
Anoint us, O God,
    with oils that never fail. Amen.

THANKSGIVING AND COMMUNION

Invitation to the Offering (1 Kings 17)

A widow in great need shared what she had, and miracles of bread and renewed life ensued. Whatever our means, whatever our needs, we each have something to share. In gratitude to God, let us offer our tithes and gifts to the One who is faithful.

Offering Prayer (Luke 7, Psalm 146)

As crowds spread the word of Jesus' power, O God,
    so may we spread the word of your grace,
        as we share these gifts and our very lives
            with those in need.

May these offerings be instruments of your healing,
> your justice, and your good news,
>> in this community and around the world.
In Christ's name we pray. Amen.

SENDING FORTH

Benediction (1 Kings 17)
Elijah was sent to someone in need—
> not only to serve,
> but that he too might also be served.
Wherever God sends you, go to serve,
> but allow others to serve you as well;
> and may the peace of Christ go with you.
Go in peace.

CONTEMPORARY OPTIONS

Contemporary Gathering Words (1 Kings 17, Psalm 146, Luke 7)
Strangers meet.
Oil and grain turn to bread.
The sick are healed.
The weary are lifted up.
The prisoners are set free.
The everyday becomes a miracle.
This is God's work.
We are its witnesses.
Let us worship God.

Praise Sentences (Psalm 146)
Praise God! Praise God, O my soul!
> **As long as I live, I will praise God!**
Praise God! Praise God, O my soul!
> **God will reign forever, for all generations!**
Praise God! Praise God, O my soul!
> **Happy are those whose help is in God!**
Praise God! Praise God, O my soul!
> **Praise God!**

JUNE 16, 2013
Fourth Sunday after Pentecost /
Father's Day

Ken Burton

COLOR
Green

SCRIPTURE READINGS
1 Kings 21:1-21a; Psalm 5:1-8; Galatians 2:15-21; Luke 7:36–8:3

THEME IDEAS
The story of Ahab, Jezebel, and Naboth depicts a God of retribution, punishing Ahab for the sins of his wife! Yet, grace emerges in both the Psalm and our New Testament readings. The letter to the Galatians proclaims life, not through the law, but as a consequence of the indwelling Christ. Luke's Gospel speaks of the fullness of redemptive love, expressed in the faith of one who has been forgiven much. While stories of a God who would punish us for the sins of another are part of our scriptural heritage, we worship a God of forgiving love.

INVITATION AND GATHERING
Call to Worship (Psalm 5)
Give ear to my words, O Lord.
Give heed to my sighing.

Listen to the sound of my cry, my King and my God.
Be present, Holy One, in this time and place.

—OR—

Call to Worship (Psalm 5)

Through the abundance of your steadfast love, O God,
we will enter your house.
Through the abundance of your steadfast love, O God,
we will bow down in awe in your holy temple.
Through the abundance of your steadfast love, O God,
we will listen to your holy word.
Through the abundance of your steadfast love, O God,
we will follow the path you lay before us.
Through the abundance of your steadfast love, O God,
we will worship you in love and gratitude.
(Rebecca Gaudino)

Opening Prayer (Psalm 5)

Faithful, forgiving Father of new beginnings,
  we enter your house this day
    surrounded by your steadfast love.
Gentle, embracing Mother of encouragement,
  we hear your voice this hour
    in the words spoken
      and the movement of the spirit
        in our hearts.
Let your will be known,
  for we would be your people,
    even as you are our God. Amen.

PROCLAMATION AND RESPONSE

Prayer of Confession (1 Kings 21, Luke 7)

Holy One,
  like Ahab before us,
    we have done what is evil in your sight;
  like the woman in the home of Simon the Pharisee,
    who anointed Jesus' feet with her tears

and dried them with her hair,
    we have much to be forgiven for.
We have ignored your voice calling us to compassion.
We have turned away
    from our homeless and hungry sisters and brothers.
We have allowed our anger to fester into rage,
    lashing out against friends and family.
We have much to be forgiven for, O God.
Hear our prayer as we plead for your healing love.

Words of Assurance (Galatians 2)
Hear the good news:
    The God who creates also forgives.
    The risen Christ offers life in his name.
    The Holy Spirit lives within,
        blessing us with love and forgiveness.
Hear the good news and be glad.
    Thanks be to God!

Response to the Word (Luke 7)
Holy One,
    we have heard your word of forgiveness and love.
As people for whom much has been forgiven,
    may we also be agents
        of great forgiveness and love. Amen.

THANKSGIVING AND COMMUNION

Invitation to the Offering (Luke 8)
As the women who traveled with Jesus provided for him
and his disciples out of their abundance, so may we give
generously from ours.

Offering Prayer
God, who loves us like a mother
    and forgives us like a father,
        we have received so much from your hand.
We offer back a portion of your gifts to us
    for your work in the church and in the world.

Bless our offerings to your use,
and bless us as we offer ourselves
to your service. Amen.

SENDING FORTH

Benediction (Galatians 2, Luke 7)
Let us go forth from this place
secure in the knowledge of God's love.
In Christ, we are forgiven.
Christ lives in us and we in him.
**We are bearers of Christ's love
to a broken and hungry world.**
This is good news indeed!

CONTEMPORARY OPTIONS

Contemporary Gathering Words (Psalm 5, Luke 7)
Holy One, listen to our cries and songs.
Love us, and forgive our wrongs.
Listen to our cries and songs.
Love us, and forgive our wrongs.

Praise Sentences (Galatians 2)
God, you made us.
Christ, you save us.
Spirit, you show us the way.
We praise you for your love and forgiveness.
God, you made us.
Christ, you save us.
Spirit, you show us the way.
We praise you for your love and forgiveness.

JUNE 23, 2013

Fifth Sunday after Pentecost

Sara Dunning Lambert

COLOR

Green

SCRIPTURE READINGS

1 Kings 19:1-15a; Psalm 42; Galatians 3:23-29; Luke 8:26-39

THEME IDEAS

The steadfast love of God is evident throughout the passages for this day. Elijah becomes the expression of resolute and determined faith, an example rewarded by God carrying him to safety. The psalmist reminds us that throughout times of distress and dark nights of the soul, God is ever present. The Epistle passage proclaims that we are justified by faith in Christ, who claims us all as children of God. The promise of belonging to Christ is echoed in the healing of the Gerasene demoniac who Jesus instructs to share how much God has done for him.

INVITATION AND GATHERING

Call to Worship (1 Kings 19, Psalm 42, Galatians 3)
We often feel as if we are wandering through our lives, searching for something we cannot name.
We come today to listen for hope, to pray for strength, and to experience God's love.

Speak to us of faith, hope, and love, O Lord.
As the deer longs for flowing water in the wilderness,
we long to drink deeply of God's promise for us.
Knowing God is here, we join together on our journey.
Lead us to your still waters, O Lord.
Imprisoned by rules of our own making,
we come to remember and claim our faith.
Assured by the vision of Christ,
whose sacrifice leads us to heaven,
we come in fellowship with one another.
Clothe us in the love of Christ, O Lord.
With shouts of praise and songs of thanksgiving,
we come to celebrate the God of hope,
the Spirit of peace, and the Christ of redeeming love.
We come to pray.
We come to sing.
We come to worship and praise.

—OR—

Call to Worship (1 Kings 19, Psalm 42, Galatians 3, Luke 8)
As the deep calls to the deep
in thundering waves of faith and steadfast love,
so we stand on the mountain with Elijah,
feeling billowing waves of God's power
flowing over and through us.
Set aside your enemies—
the people, thoughts, time, and challenges—
that separate you from knowing God's love.
Clothe yourselves in Christ.
Shout praise in his name,
and declare how much God has done for you.

Opening Prayer (1 Kings 19)
God of mystery,
open our eyes,
to look for you in unfamiliar places;
open our ears,

to hear you speak in the sound
    of sheer silence;
open our hearts,
    to feel the depth of your love.
When we wander in the wilderness of fear and death,
    revive us with your care,
        that we may find strength for our journey
        back to the land of hope and life. Amen.
(B. J. Beu)

PROCLAMATION AND RESPONSE

Prayer of Confession (1 Kings 19, Psalm 42, Galatians 3)

Lord of the ages,
    in our busy lives,
        we do not always make time to love, to pray,
        or to sing your praises.
We want to be strong,
    yet we often feel out of control:
        buffeted by the winds of change,
        rocked by the earthquakes in our relationships,
        burned by the fires of doubt.
Forgetting what we cannot see,
    we ask, "Why have you forgotten me?"
Help us trust your presence,
    even when we feel utterly alone,
        trapped in our dark night of the soul.
With the promise of Christ as our hope,
    lead us from our own wilderness wanderings
        into the well-tended garden of your love.

Words of Assurance (Psalm 42, Galatians 3)

The steadfast love of God is with you—
    yesterday, today, and tomorrow.
Whether you turn away or doubt,
    whether you follow timidly or joyfully,
    you are loved and forgiven in Christ.

Passing the Peace of Christ

May you know the peace of Christ in the midst of suffering. May you feel the hope of the Holy Spirit in the midst of sorrow. And may you touch the love of God in the midst of pain. Feel God's love blowing through your life, as you turn to one another and pass the peace of Christ.

Prayer of Preparation (Psalm 42, Galatians 3)

Holy One, prepare us to receive your word. As we listen in faith and hope, open our souls to your quenching waters. Free us from the confinement of our hearts, that we may hear the promise of your love.

Response to the Word (Psalm 42, Galatians 3, Luke 8)

Justified by faith,
> we are clothed in Christ.

Sanctified by the Spirit,
> we are one in God with one another.

We place our hope in God—
> praising God's help and love,
> declaring how much God has done for us.

THANKSGIVING AND COMMUNION

Invitation to the Offering (1 Kings 19, Psalm 42, Galatians 3)

Be zealous in shouting your praises to the Lord. Remembering the strength of God's love and the promise of Christ's help, let us share who we are as the church in the world. With open arms, let us join with one another as we express our faith through our gifts of love.

Offering Prayer (1 Kings 19, Luke 8)

Sovereign God,
> you feed us by your own hand,
>> lest our souls shrivel
>>> for want of nourishment;

you revive us with the waters of life,
   lest our hearts faint
      in the desert of our despair;
you call us back to life and new possibilities,
   lest our hopes fail
      in our sorrow and anguish.
Accept these offerings,
   in gratitude and praise,
      for the many blessings
         we have received from your hand.
Accept the gift of our love,
   and our pledge to love others
      as you have loved us. Amen.
(B. J. Beu)

SENDING FORTH

Benediction (1 Kings 19, Psalm 42, Galatians 3, Luke 8)
In the spirit of God's unchanging love,
   live the stories of faith we have heard this day.
In the melody of God's song within us,
   sing the faith we have received this day.
In the hope of God's unfailing help,
   share the grace we have touched this day.
Go and tell the world how much God has done for us!

CONTEMPORARY OPTIONS

Contemporary Gathering Words (1 Kings 19, Psalm 42)
Praise the God of Elijah,
who is steadfast and strong in the wilderness.
   Our hope is in God!
Praise the God of the lost,
who is our rock and our help in times of need.
   Our help is in God!
Praise the God of Jesus Christ,
who makes us children of the beloved.
   Our life is in Christ! Amen!

Praise Sentences (Psalm 42, Galatians 3)
The steadfast love of the Lord lasts forever!
The unfailing hope of the Lord
  is like prayer and song in the heart.
Clothed in Christ,
  we are justified by faith.
Belonging to Christ, we are one in him,
  promised as children of Abraham
  to inherit God's love.

Praise Sentences (Psalm 42)
Hope in God, our rock and our help.
Hope in God, our living water in the desert.
Hope in God, our song of praise.
Hope in God, our rock and our help.
(B. J. Beu)

JUNE 30, 2013

Sixth Sunday after Pentecost

B. J. Beu

COLOR

Green

SCRIPTURE READINGS

2 Kings 2:1-2, 6-14; Psalm 77:1-2, 11-20; Galatians 5:1, 13-25; Luke 9:51-62

THEME IDEAS

No matter how much we don't want it to happen, no matter how unprepared we feel to be on our own, mentors and guides eventually leave us, forcing us to carry on without them. Elisha follows Elijah until the very end when his mentor and master is carried away in the whirlwind, for Elisha knows he cannot follow in the great prophet's footsteps without a double portion of Elijah's spirit. Jesus sets his face toward Jerusalem, knowing there is no return. The disciples will soon feel this loss. The psalmist cries out to God in distress, remembering God's great capacity to make everything right again. Galatians does not fit into this theme, but beautifully describes the fruit of the Spirit available to those who live by the Spirit—as Elijah, Elisha, and Jesus did; indeed, as we do when we love our neighbor as we love ourselves.

INVITATION AND GATHERING

Call to Worship *(2 Kings 2, Galatians 5, Luke 9)*

Christ says, "Follow me."
We're almost ready.
Christ says, "Bear fruit of the Spirit."
We're waiting for the harvest.
Christ says, "Pick up my mantle
and proclaim my name."
We're a little tongue-tied.
Trust the one who calls you. You are ready.
We will not leave you, Lord. Lead on.

Opening Prayer *(2 Kings 2, Psalm 77, Luke 9)*

Mighty God,
   your voice is like the crash of thunder,
      your breath is like a whirlwind
         that breaks the mighty cedars
            as though they were twigs.
Come to us, Holy One,
   when we have need of you,
      when we feel abandoned and alone.
For you alone can comfort us,
   and lead us through the waters of grief and loss.
You alone can send us the help we need
   to cross over to other shores,
      and find our way home.
Give us the courage of Elisha,
   to ask for a double portion of your Spirit,
      for we cannot go it alone.
In your faithful name, we pray. Amen.

PROCLAMATION AND RESPONSE

Prayer of Confession *(Galatians 5)*

Gracious God,
   you offer us freedom in Christ,
      promising us the fruit of the Spirit

if we would but live in your Spirit,
but we settle for slavery to our baser instincts,
giving ourselves over to self-indulgence
and earthly appetites.
Forgive us when we choose to devour one another,
rather than to love our neighbor as ourselves.
Help us claim our godly inheritance,
that our lives may bear the fruit of your Spirit:
love, joy, peace, patience, kindness, generosity,
faithfulness, gentleness, and self-control.
In this we will find life,
and the freedom you offer us in Christ. Amen.

Words of Assurance (Galatians 5)

If we live by the Spirit,
we will be guided by the Spirit—
we will know the grace that comes
from life in Christ.
Christ came to set us free.
Christ set us free that we might have life
and have it abundantly.
Rejoice in God's love and forgiveness.

Passing the Peace of Christ (Galatians 5)

The fruit of the Spirit is peace. Share this peace with one
another in joy and thanksgiving as we celebrate freedom
in Christ.

Response to the Word (Galatians 5)

The fruit of the Spirit is love, joy, and peace.
Give us this fruit always, O God.
The fruit of the Spirit is patience, kindness,
and generosity.
Feed us with your Spirit, Holy One.
The fruit of the Spirit is faithfulness, gentleness,
and self-control.
Lead us to life, Spirit of the living God.
Lead on.

THANKSGIVING AND COMMUNION

Offering Prayer (2 Kings 2, Galatians 5)
You always give us the freedom to turn back, O Lord,
    to take an easier road.
But when we have the strength to carry on
    and ask for a double portion of your Spirit,
        like Elisha before us,
            we find blessing upon blessing.
May these gifts reflect our gratitude
    for your many gifts,
        especially your fruit of the Spirit.
May these gifts lift up others in their need,
    that they may see their own freedom
        to choose life. Amen.

SENDING FORTH

Benediction (Galatians 5, Luke 9)
May the freedom you find in Christ
    and the transforming love of God
        work within you to produce fruit of the Spirit.
Relish the sweet taste of love, joy, peace, patience,
    kindness, generosity, faithfulness, and self-control.
Love your neighbor as you love yourself,
    and you will touch eternal life each and every day.
Go with God.

CONTEMPORARY OPTIONS

Contemporary Gathering Words (2 Kings 2, Luke 9)
We are people of the Spirit—
    people of God's whirlwind,
    people of fiery horses and chariots.
We are heirs with Christ—
    heirs of freedom,
    heirs of a love that will not let us go.
We are people of God—

people of promise,
people of glorious hope.
Thanks be to God!

Praise Sentences (Galatians 5, Luke 9)
The fruit of the Spirit is love.
The fruit of the Spirit is joy.
The fruit of the Spirit is peace.
The fruit of the Spirit is all this and so much more.
Praise God for the Spirit.
Praise God for life.
Praise God for the Spirit!
Praise God for life!

JULY 7, 2013

Seventh Sunday after Pentecost

B. J. Beu

COLOR

Green

SCRIPTURE READINGS

2 Kings 5:1-14; Psalm 30; Galatians 6:(1-6) 7-16; Luke 10:1-11, 16-20

THEME IDEAS

A young captive from the land of Israel sends her master Naaman back to her homeland to be healed of his leprosy. Another foreign servant convinces Naaman to do as Elisha bids in order that he may be made clean. Jesus sends seventy followers out to share God's blessings and peace, knowing he is sending them out "like lambs into the midst of wolves" (Luke 10:3). Galatians urges us to correct transgressors in a spirit of gentleness. True power, godly power, seems to come from those who have every reason to withhold it. God is here to save us, but mysteriously works through the most unexpected sources.

INVITATION AND GATHERING

Call to Worship (Psalm 30)
Sing praises to the Lord, O faithful ones.
Give thanks to God's holy name.

God has turned our mourning into dancing,
our weeping into shouts of joy.
Rejoice and be glad, O people of God.
Extol God's holy name.
God's anger may last a moment,
but God's favor endures a lifetime.
Sing praises forever, O treasured ones.
Proclaim the good news of God's favor.
God has taken off our sackcloth
and clothed us with joy.

Opening Prayer or Benediction (2 Kings 5, Galatians 6, Luke 10)

Lift up our hearts, O God,
that we may seek the welfare of all.
Bathe us in healing waters,
that we may be washed clean.
Send us forth with messages of peace,
that others may know of your gentle love.
Lead us into life,
that we may be made new in your Spirit. Amen.

PROCLAMATION AND RESPONSE

Prayer of Confession (2 Kings 5, Galatians 6, Luke 10)

Mysterious One,
you send us into the world,
like lambs into the midst of wolves,
to proclaim your peace;
you move within our hearts,
stirring us to seek the welfare
of those who have done us harm;
you instruct us reach out in gentleness
to those who have gone astray.
Sometimes, O God, we do not feel up to it.
It is hard to love our nation's enemy.
It is difficult to heal those
who have advocated violence.

It is humbling to learn of your love
    for those we have been taught to despise.
Forgive us.
Teach us anew to follow your ways,
    that we too may be made whole. Amen.

Words of Assurance (Psalm 30)

God's anger may last a moment,
    but God's favor lasts a lifetime.
Weeping may last the night,
    but joy comes in the morning.
Rejoice and be glad,
    for we worship a God of steadfast love.
In the mercy of God, we are forgiven.

Passing the Peace of Christ (Luke 10)

Just as Jesus sent his disciples into the world to share words of peace, let us greet one another with words of peace this day. Turn to your neighbor and share signs of peace with these words: "The peace of Christ be with you."

Response to the Word (Galatians 6)

God does not call the equipped,
    God equips those who are called.
Know that God has equipped us
    as laborers in the fields of God's harvest.
With gentleness and words of peace,
    look to the welfare of all. Amen.

THANKSGIVING AND COMMUNION

Offering Prayer (Galatians 6)

Bountiful God,
    you promise that we will reap
        what we sow.
May today's offering
    reflect our commitment in Christ
        to sow in the Spirit.

Transform our gifts
into labors of gentleness and peace,
that the world may touch your love. Amen.

SENDING FORTH

Benediction (Galatians 6, Luke 10)
Bear one another's burdens.
Correct one another with gentleness.
Bless one another with signs of peace.
Do not grow weary in doing what is right
and you will reap a rich harvest
of joy, hope, and love.
Go in the peace of the Lord.

CONTEMPORARY OPTIONS

Contemporary Gathering Words (Galatians 6, Luke 10)
Can you hear it? God is speaking.
Where? How?
Can you perceive it? Christ offers us peace.
Are you kidding?
We're too stressed to feel anything.
God speaks through us.
God offers peace through the words on our lips.
It can't be that simple.
It's always that simple.
That's why it's so hard.
Work through us, Lord,
your servants are here.

Praise Sentences (Psalm 30, Luke 10)
Sing praises to the Lord, sing praises.
God replaces our tears with shouts of joy.
Sing praises to the Lord, sing praises.
God turns our mourning into dancing.
Sing praises to the Lord, sing praises.
God writes our names in the book of life.

JULY 14, 2013

Eighth Sunday after Pentecost

B. J. Beu

COLOR

Green

SCRIPTURE READINGS

Amos 7:7-17; Psalm 82; Colossians 1:1-14; Luke 10:25-37

THEME IDEAS

Divine and human judgment focus these readings. God uses a plumb line in Amos to judge Israel, finding it wanting. The psalmist calls upon God to take up the roll of judge once again, wondering whether God has ignored the sins of the wicked and the powerful to the detriment of the weak and the orphan. Paul has heard of the faith of the Colossians and has judged them worthy of their calling. Faithfulness leads to growth in grace, love, truth, and life. Asked by a lawyer, "Who is my neighbor?" Jesus tells the well-known parable of the Good Samaritan and asks the man to judge for himself who a neighbor is. Although we often react negatively to the idea of judging, these passages make clear that sound judgment can be a righteous enterprise. We are called to righteous judgment, without becoming judgmental.

INVITATION AND GATHERING

Call to Worship (Psalm 82)

Shout to the Lord, O people of God.
Make plain your petitions before the judgment seat.
God hears our cries and rescues the perishing,
maintaining the right of the lowly and destitute.
Call to the Lord, O disciples of the Holy One.
Proclaim your case before God's holy council.
God hearkens to our call and rescues the weak,
lifting up the widow and the orphan.
Sing to the Lord, O children of the Most High.
Express your need before the judge of all the earth.
God listens to our pleas and heals our wounds,
filling our darkness with life-giving light.

—OR—

Call to Worship (Luke 10)

God offers us eternal life.
We will love the Lord our God,
with all our heart, with all our soul,
with all our mind, and with all our strength.
God calls us to love one another.
We will love our neighbor as we love ourselves.
Worship the God of abundant love.

Opening Prayer (Colossians 1, Luke 10)

God of power and might,
your saints have ever lived
in the glory of your love.
Fill us with your grace and peace,
that we may know the richness
of eternal life in your Spirit.
Help us love you with all our heart,
with all our soul, with all our strength,
and with all our mind;
even as we love our neighbor
as we love ourselves.

For only in loving, Holy One,
    do we lead lives worthy of your calling,
        through Jesus Christ, our Lord. Amen.

PROCLAMATION AND RESPONSE

Prayer of Confession (Amos 7, Psalm 82, Colossians 1, Luke 10)
Your judgment, Holy One,
    reveals us for who we truly are.
We do not always like what we see.
Judged against the plumb line of your justice,
    our ways seem out of balance,
    our practices seem wanting.
Forgive us, Most High:
    when we show partiality to the powerful,
    when we deny justice to the weak and destitute,
    when we ignore the cry of the widow and orphan,
    when we turn a blind eye to the wicked.
We know what it takes to taste the fruit of eternal life,
    but we can't seem to make ourselves reach out
        and taste its sweetness, right here, right now.
We know what it means to be a good neighbor,
    but we can't seem to bring ourselves to be one.
Work within us, O God,
    as you worked in the saints of old,
        that our works may bear good fruit
        and our lives may shine the light
        of your justice. Amen.

Words of Assurance (Colossians 1)
In Christ, we have been made strong,
    through the strength of God's glorious power.
For God has rescued us from the power of darkness
    to shine forth with the light of Christ.
Rejoice, for in Christ, we are forgiven.

Passing the Peace of Christ (Colossians 1)
There is no greater gift than sharing God's grace and
peace. There is no greater honor than receiving these gifts

175

from another. With thankful hearts, turn to one another
now and share signs of God's grace and peace.

Response to the Word or Benediction (Colossians 1, Luke 10)

We hear God's word with more than the hope
   that there is treasure laid up for us in heaven.
We hear with the promise of eternal life—
   life that begins right here, right now:
      when we love God with all our heart,
      with all of our soul,
      with all of our strength,
      and with all of our mind;
   life that begins when we love our neighbor
      as we love ourselves.
Love well and you will live.

THANKSGIVING AND COMMUNION

Offering Prayer (Psalm 82, Colossians 1, Luke 10)

Bountiful God,
   your word bears the fruit of hope and grace;
   your ways lead to fullness of life.
May today's offering bear fruit in our world,
   that old hatreds may cease,
      old wounds may be healed,
         and old divisions may be mended.
Through our gifts,
   may the weak and the needy find justice,
      may the widow and orphan find support,
         and may the afflicted find solace. Amen.

SENDING FORTH

Benediction (Psalm 82, Colossians 1, Luke 10)

Go forth in the strength of God's glorious power.
We will live in the light of God's ways.
Go forth in the hope of lives lived in Christ.
We will bear the fruit of life in Christ.

Go forth in the power of God's Holy Spirit.
**We will judge others with spiritual wisdom
and holy understanding.**
Go with God.

CONTEMPORARY OPTIONS

Contemporary Gathering Words (Luke 10)
What must we do to inherit eternal life?
Tell us what the Bible teaches.
You shall love the Lord your God
with all your heart, and with all your soul,
and with all your strength, and with all your mind.
And you shall love your neighbor as yourself.
We can love God, but our neighbor...
Just who is our neighbor anyway?
That's the wrong question.
What's the right question then?
How can we be good neighbors.
Tell us what the Bible teaches.
Show mercy, even for enemies.
Show kindness and compassion for those in need,
even those we don't like.
This isn't getting any easier.
The way of the Lord isn't easy,
but it's the only way that leads to life.
Teach us Lord. Your servants are listening.

Praise Sentences (Luke 10)
Love God with all your heart.
Praise God for life.
Love God with all your soul.
Praise God for life eternal.
Love God with all your strength.
Praise God for life everlasting.
Love God with all your mind.
Praise God for life in Christ.

JULY 21, 2013

Ninth Sunday after Pentecost
Leigh Anne Taylor

COLOR

Green

SCRIPTURE READINGS

Amos 8:1-12; Psalm 52; Colossians 1:15-28; Luke 10:38-42

THEME IDEAS

Amos and the psalmist offer harsh judgment against evil-doers—those who take advantage of the poor, those who lie and cheat. Paul offers the radical message to the Colossians that those who were previously considered unworthy (Gentiles and evildoers) are reconciled to God through Christ's death. In his welcome and approval of Mary as student and disciple, Jesus makes it clear that women are worthy in God's kingdom too. The good news is that Christ welcomes all and dwells within all who have steadfast faith.

Call to Worship (Psalm 52)

All who love the Lord, draw near.
> **Like green olive trees in the house of the Lord,**
> **we will trust in the steadfast love of God,**
> **forever and ever.**

All who love the Lord our God, draw near.
> **We will thank the Lord forever,**
> **because of what the mighty One has done.**

All who love the Lord our God, draw near to worship.
In the presence of the faithful,
we will proclaim God's name, for it is good.

Opening Prayer or Prayer of Confession (Luke 10,
Amos 8, Colossians 1)
Day by day,
our lives are filled with many distractions.
Hour by hour,
our lives are preoccupied with endless tasks.
Jesus Christ, we have come on this day, in this hour,
to leave behind our cares and burdens
and fill our lives with your presence.
In gratitude for the feast that you spread before us,
in the richness of your word,
we choose the better part,
of listening at your feet,
that your word would dwell within us,
for the sake of your glory. Amen.

PROCLAMATION AND RESPONSE

Prayer of Confession (Amos 8, Psalm 52, Colossians 1)
Loving God,
your gift of abundant life
is like a basket of summer fruit:
full to overflowing,
ripe and ready for us to enjoy;
but the life we choose
more closely resembles a bowl of plastic fruit:
beautiful to look at
but utterly empty and unsatisfying.
We have been careless to the needs of others.
We have been self-centered,
cheating the powerless and the poor,
seeking refuge in our wealth and possessions.
We have loved evil more than good,
being blinded by our own self-interest.

Forgive us, merciful God.
Recreate us anew,
    and fill us with the gift of your abundant life. Amen.

Words of Assurance (Colossians 1)

Hear the good news:
    Though we were once estranged from God
    we are now reconciled to the Holy One,
    presented holy and blameless,
    through Christ's reconciling love.
Let us stand firm in our faith in Jesus Christ,
    receiving forgiveness and the gift of abundant life
    in his name.

Passing the Peace of Christ (Colossians 1)

We have the great gift of peace because we have been reconciled to God through Christ. With thanksgiving to God, let us offer one another signs of peace and reconciliation.

Introduction to the Word or Prayer of Preparation (Luke 10)

The teacher is here. Pull up a chair. There's a place for you in the front row. Listen. Take notes. Pay close attention to what the teacher is saying to you today.

Response to the Word (Colossians 1)

This is the word of God for the people of God.
**May the word of God be made fully known
in us today.**

THANKSGIVING AND COMMUNION

Offering Prayer (Amos 8)

Loving God,
    you fill our lives with such abundant gifts
        that we are filled to overflowing
            like baskets of summer fruit.
From our gratitude to you,
    and our love for our neighbors,
        we return now a portion of these gifts to you.

May these gifts honor you,
   and may those who receive them
      know the richness of your love. Amen.

SENDING FORTH

Benediction (Colossians 1)
This is the mystery that has been revealed to us:
Christ lives within us.
   Christ lives in us when we have faith in him.
Go now to see Christ in everyone you meet.
   We go to love our neighbor
   as Christ has loved us.

CONTEMPORARY OPTIONS

Contemporary Gathering Words (Colossians 1, Psalm 52)
Before Christ, we were far from God
   and stuck in our evil ways.
Through Christ's life and death,
   we are brought close to God again
   and our slate was wiped clean.
Listen to the good news: Have faith in Christ
   and Christ will live in you!
Praise God for all God has done for us!

Praise Sentences (Colossians 1, Psalm 52)
Have faith in Christ.
Hold on to it and never let it go.
Christ will live in you!
God is so good!
I will thank God forever for what God has done for us.

JULY 28, 2013

Tenth Sunday after Pentecost
Deborah Sokolove

COLOR
Green

SCRIPTURE READINGS
Hosea 1:2-10; Psalm 85; Colossians 2:6-15 (16-19); Luke 11:1-13

THEME IDEAS
God offers love, compassion, and forgiveness to all who come in repentance and prayer. Through following the teachings of Jesus, we learn to ask God to give us what we really need.

Call to Worship (Hosea 1, Luke 11)
Ask, and it will be given you.
Search, and you will find.
Knock, and the door will be opened for you.
We knock on the door of heaven.
For everyone who asks receives.
Everyone who searches finds.
And for everyone who knocks,
the door will be opened.
We ask for the bread of salvation.
Just as we yearn to give good gifts to our children,
so the Holy One yearns to give us good gifts,
welcoming all who come as children

of the Living God.
We seek the God who calls us.

Opening Prayer (Luke 11)
God of all that is and yet shall be,
    you are father and mother to all your children,
        giving us good gifts—
            gifts of life, love, and compassion.
Although we often lose our way,
    you continue to gather us into your arms
        and feed us with the bread of heaven.
Open our hearts and fill us with your Holy Spirit,
    that we may bring the love of Jesus
        to a weary and broken world. Amen.

PROCLAMATION AND RESPONSE

Prayer of Confession (Hosea 1, Colossians 2, Luke 11)
God of compassion and justice,
    forgive our many shortcomings.
We have not always been a faithful church.
We have forgotten our baptismal vows,
    taken in by the lies of the world.
We have refused to share what we have with others,
    giving scorpions instead of eggs,
    and snakes instead of fish,
        to those in need.
We have held grudges against those who have hurt us,
    ignoring our own faults,
        and denying our responsibility
            for the hurts we have caused others.
Help us turn away from sin,
    to become once again your holy people.

Words of Assurance (Psalm 85)
Steadfast love and faithfulness will meet,
    and righteousness and peace will kiss.
Faithfulness will spring up from the ground,
    and righteousness will look down from the sky.

The Holy One gives what is good,
    forgiving our sins and holding us in love.
In the name of Christ, you are forgiven.
In the name of Christ, you are forgiven.
Thanks be to God.

Passing the Peace of Christ (Luke 11)

In joyful thanks for God's loving compassion, let us exchange signs of peace.
May the peace of Christ be with you.
The peace of Christ be with you always.

Prayer of Preparation (Luke 11)

Holy One,
    like the disciples who did not know how to pray,
      we ask that you open the door
        of our understanding,
          and feed us with the bread
            of your holy word. Amen.

Response to the Word (Hosea 1, Luke 11)

Living, loving God,
    like the disciples who did not know how to pray,
    you have shown us how to ask for the good gifts
      you have prepared for us.
We give you thanks for making us your children
and feeding us with the bread of salvation.

THANKSGIVING AND COMMUNION

Offering Prayer (Luke 11)

Generous Source of breath and life,
    like the friend who rises at midnight,
      you open the door when we knock
        and fill our hands with good gifts.
Receive these tokens of our gratitude and joy,
that they may fill the empty hands
that reach out to you still. Amen.

Invitation to Communion (Colossians 2, Luke 11)
At the table of Christ, everyone who asks will receive; everyone who is searching will find; and for everyone who knocks, the door will be opened. Do not let anyone or anything keep you away, for this is the table of the heavenly feast. A place is set for all who want to follow Jesus into new life.

SENDING FORTH

Benediction (Hosea 1, Luke 11)
Go from this place as children of the Living God,
    bearing the love and compassion of Christ
    and the power of the Holy Spirit
    into a hungry and hurting world.

CONTEMPORARY OPTIONS

Contemporary Gathering Words (Luke 11)
Ask, and it will be given you.
Search, and you will find.
Knock, and the door will be opened for you.
    For everyone who asks receives,
    and everyone who searches finds,
    and for everyone who knocks,
    the door will be opened.

Praise Sentences (Psalm 85)
Salvation is at hand for those who turn to God.
    Faithfulness will spring up from the ground,
    and righteousness will look down from the sky.
The Holy One gives us what is good.
    The One who is faithful
    holds us in compassionate love.

AUGUST 4, 2013

Eleventh Sunday after Pentecost
J. Wayne Pratt

COLOR
Green

SCRIPTURE READINGS
Hosea 11:1-11; Psalm 107:1-9, 43; Colossians 3:1-11; Luke 12:13-21

THEME IDEAS
These readings starkly contrast a life of reliance on wealth with a life of dependence upon God and God's abundant blessings. Hosea prophesies judgment against Israel's idolatry and unfaithfulness; yet from a loving parent, forgiveness is offered and deliverance is promised. The psalmist calls for praise and thanksgiving in response to the Lord's abundant acts of love on behalf of God's people. Colossians reveals that through Christ's life in us, Christians are called to seek the values of heaven over the values of earth. Greed in any form is to be avoided. Because we are the same in Christ, we are to discover our life in Christ and seek to become like God. In the parable of the rich fool, Matthew likewise offers a warning against greed. Although the wealthy man feels secure and comfortable in his earthly riches, such wealth becomes meaningless in death. Christ challenges his followers to seek a rich relationship with God instead of material wealth.

INVITATION AND GATHERING

Call to Worship (Psalm 107, Luke 12)
O give thanks to the Lord, for God is good.
God's love and warm embrace last forever.
When we cry out in distress, the Lord hears our call.
Praise the Lord who delivers us
from sin and death.
Christ calls us to clothe ourselves in righteousness.
Worship the One who wraps us with justice,
and helps us grow in the image of our Creator.
Love well, for your heart is where your treasure is.
May our hearts be filled with God's blessings,
divine provisions that meet our true needs.

Opening Prayer (Hosea 11, Psalm 107)
Loving and Forgiving God,
be present with us now,
as we offer praise and thanksgiving
for the abundance we have received
though your grace.
You have gathered us in,
from the east and from the west,
from the north and from the south,
to be your people.
Like a loving Parent,
you have sustained our needs—
sharing your love with us,
satisfying our thirst,
and filling our hunger with good things.
Help us, Lord, to heed your call,
that we might find deliverance
through Christ Jesus, our Lord and Savior.

PROCLAMATION AND RESPONSE

Prayer of Confession (Colossians 3, Matthew 12)
Gracious God,
in our wanderings and selfish desires:

we have forsaken fellowship with our families,
    our friends, and our neighbors;
we have neglected our communion with you,
    choosing worldly pleasures and desires
        over truth, justice, and righteousness.
In a world of plenty,
    we have hoarded our earthly blessings,
        rather than storing up our heavenly treasures.
Free us from such bondage,
    that we may truly reveal
        the presence of Christ in our lives. Amen.

Words of Assurance (Colossians 3)

In faith, we call out to a loving and forgiving God,
    seeking to put aside our old life and put on Christ.
God surely answers our prayers.
In the name of Christ Jesus, our sins are forgiven.
    Thanks be to God.

Passing the Peace of Christ

"Peace I leave with you," said Jesus. Let us now share this
extravagant gift with one another.
The peace of Christ be with you.
    And also with you.

Prayer of Preparation (Psalm 107, Colossians 3, Luke 12)

Loving Lord,
    open our hearts this day,
        as we proclaim your holy word.
As we offer praise and thanksgiving,
    in response to your abundant acts of love,
    challenge us to seek the values of heaven
        over the trappings of this world.
May the words we experience this day
    call us to a rich relationship with you,
    as we learn to live out the calling of our baptism,
        through Jesus Christ our Lord. Amen.

Response to the Word (Colossians 3)

God of love and grace,
   send your Spirit upon us
      that we may not only hear your words,
         but find creative and faithful ways
           to put them into action.
Help us, Lord, to be people of compassion,
   living out our baptism
      as we put on Christ
         and turn our hearts to you. Amen.

THANKSGIVING AND COMMUNION

Invitation to the Offering (Luke 12)

Prosperity is given to the greater community of believers, so that all of God's children may benefit. Let us demonstrate that we are the body of Christ through our extravagant sharing of God's blessings this day. And let us give out of our joy, rather than out of a sense of obligation, as we offer to our God the gifts of our hearts.

Offering Prayer (Luke 12)

O God,
   we stand before you as a people of faith,
      investing our lives and our treasures
         for the glory of your kingdom.
Bless these gifts and those who gave them,
   in Jesus' precious name. Amen.

SENDING FORTH

Benediction (Luke 12, Colossians 3)

Happy are those who know real treasure
and where to find it.
   Happy are those who receive God's treasure
   and share it unselfishly.
Invest your life and your heart in Christ,
just as God has invested Christ in you.

Happy are those whose reward
is found in heaven, not on earth.
Go now in the name of Christ,
God's ultimate gift of love.
Thanks be to God.

CONTEMPORARY OPTIONS

Contemporary Gathering Words (Colossians 3)

If we have been raised with Christ Jesus,
let us set our minds on heavenly things,
not on the things that are on earth.
The old self is gone.
Let us revel in the Spirit
that strips away the trappings of death,
and dresses us in garments that are new.
As new creations in God,
we are separated and divided no longer.
Christ is all and in all!
Thanks be to God.

Praise Sentences (Psalm 107)

Give thanks to the Lord, for God is good.
God's steadfast love endures forever.
Those who are wise give heed to these things,
for the Lord is steadfast and true.
The Lord is steadfast and true.
The Lord is steadfast and true.

AUGUST 11, 2013

Twelfth Sunday after Pentecost
Robin D. Dillon

COLOR
Green

SCRIPTURE READINGS
Isaiah 1:1, 10-20; Psalm 50:1-8, 22-23; Hebrews 11:1-3, 8-16; Luke 12:32-40

THEME IDEAS
Eschatology focuses this week's readings as we contemplate the coming of God's reign. Isaiah warns that God is not pleased with hollow worship and sacrifice. One must be cleansed by ceasing to do evil and by seeking justice. Likewise, the psalmist proclaims that salvation will be given to those whose sacrifice is praise and thanksgiving. In Hebrews, we are reminded of our ancestors' faith in things unseen, and of their hope in that which is yet to come. Luke tells us that God takes pleasure in opening God's realm to us. We must be alert, therefore, and ready to take action. God's reign is both here already and not yet fully realized. Such is the challenge of faith.

INVITATION AND GATHERING

Call to Worship (Psalm 50, Hebrews 11)
God called Abraham and Sarah
and promised to bless them.

Through faith they obeyed
and received God's inheritance.
God called Isaac and Jacob as heirs of that promise.
They too followed in faith, seeking God's realm.
God calls us to join them and be heirs with the faithful.
We come here in faith and are assured by hope.

Opening Prayer (Isaiah 1, Luke 12)

God of Light and Love,
who delights in all of creation,
ignite our spirits to worship with sincerity;
illumine our minds with the truth of your word;
inspire our hearts to seek only your treasure,
that we might be moved to action
and share your love.
Through Jesus Christ,
our hope and promise, we pray. Amen.

PROCLAMATION AND RESPONSE

Prayer of Confession (Isaiah 1, Luke 12)

God of unfailing love,
you ask us to share our wealth with those in need,
yet we hoard our possessions
and guard our wealth;
you call us to rescue the oppressed,
defend the orphan, and plead for the widow,
yet our pursuits are often self-serving,
ignoring those in need of our care.
Forgive us and cleanse us, O God.
Move us to be a people of justice
and propel us on the path of love. Amen.

Words of Assurance (Isaiah 1, Luke 12)

Though our sins are like scarlet, do not be afraid,
for God has washed us clean.
The Lord takes pleasure in opening God's realm to us.
Rejoice and come in!

Passing the Peace of Christ (Luke 12)
Through Christ, God's realm has been opened to us. We enter that realm, here and now, when we offer signs of love and peace to one another. Greet one another in the name of the Lord.

Introduction to the Word (Isaiah 1, Luke 12)
Hear the word of the Lord. Listen to the teaching of our God. This indeed is our treasure. May it light our paths and make us ready to take action.

Response to the Word (Luke 12, Hebrews 11)
God, you come to us at unexpected times
    and in unexpected places.
With our lamps lit,
    we will walk by faith. Amen.

THANKSGIVING AND COMMUNION

Offering Prayer (Isaiah 1, Luke 12)
Generous God,
    you offer us unfailing treasure in heaven.
In love and gratitude for your gifts to us,
    we return these gifts and offerings to you.
Use them and stretch them
    for the poor and the widow,
        the orphan and the downtrodden.
Use and stretch us,
    to do good, to seek justice,
        and to be your light in the world. Amen.

SENDING FORTH

Benediction (Luke 12, Hebrews 11)
Go forth in faith with your lamps lit,
    dressed for action.
Offer Christ's love to the world,
    that you may be a blessings to all you meet.

CONTEMPORARY OPTIONS

Contemporary Gathering Words (Psalm 50, Luke 12)

God said, "Gather to me my faithful ones."
We gather to praise and give thanks.
Jesus said, "Do not be afraid,
God gives us the kingdom."
We gather to praise and give thanks.
God speaks and summons us to worship.
We gather to praise and give thanks.

Praise Sentences (Psalm 50)

The heavens declare God's righteousness.
We honor God with our praise.
The heavens declare God's righteousness.
We honor God with our praise.

AUGUST 18, 2013

Thirteenth Sunday after Pentecost
Sara Dunning Lambert

COLOR
Green

SCRIPTURE READINGS
Isaiah 5:1-7; Psalm 80:1-2, 8-19; Hebrews 11:29–12:2; Luke 12:49-56

THEME IDEAS
The image of the vineyard becomes a metaphor for the people of God—human, flawed, willful, and contrary. Then, as now, we may find ourselves resentful of our need for God's strong, nurturing, and judging hand. We cry out in pain, feeling abandoned. Yet, when we ask for help, God is there. Hebrews' "great cloud of witnesses" directs us to look to Jesus as our example, our hope and our redeemer.

INVITATION AND GATHERING

Call to Worship (Isaiah 5, Psalm 80, Hebrews 11, Luke 12)
God of the ages, we sing your praises
in the vineyards of our lives.
   Tend the garden of our love.
Where we have become ragged and wild,
prune us in the way we should grow.

Nurture the soil of our hope.
Let your hand be upon us, leading us to Jesus,
the perfecter of our faith.
Heal the roots of our faith.
Bring us rain in drought, shade in scorching heat,
and protection in the wilderness.
Protect the growth of our spirit. Amen.

Opening Prayer (Isaiah 5, Hebrews 11, Luke 12)
Lord of the vineyard,
 we ask for your presence
  and your guidance.
In your holy wisdom,
 tend the vines of our hearts.
Teach us your righteousness,
 that our lives may flower with justice.
We come as wild grapes,
 yearning to grow fruitful in your love.
Show us the way, through Jesus your Son,
 to discern your will, hear your word,
  and grow in your ways,
   as we deepen the roots of our faith.

8/23/20

PROCLAMATION AND RESPONSE

Prayer of Confession (Isaiah 5, Psalm 80, Hebrews 11)
Divine God,
 we try to grow happily, patiently, and faithfully
  in the soil you have prepared for us.
You feed us, shelter us,
 and provide for our daily needs.
Yet, we often fail to offer you
 the fruit of our harvest.
We act as though we were abandoned children,
 trying to make it on our own.
We feel forsaken, attacked by wild boars,
 cut down by our enemies, and neglected
  in the wilderness of our lives.

Yet, through it all,
>you remain faithful.
Renew our lives once more,
>and we will call your name on high.

Words of Assurance (Isaiah 5, Psalm 80, Hebrews 11)
Be assured that God's love is sufficient.
In the warmth of the sun, the fertility of the soil,
>and the refreshment of life-giving water,
>we have been given all that we need.
God hears our cries, and comes to save us.
Through Christ we may lay aside our sins;
>through Christ, we know we are safe.

Response to the Word (Isaiah 5, Psalm 80, Hebrews 11)
While we may bear wild grapes, going astray in the world, God remains faithful. We call upon God's help today, sure in the knowledge that it will come.

THANKSGIVING AND COMMUNION

Offering Prayer (Isaiah 5, Psalm 80, Hebrews 11)
Loving Gardener,
>we offer ourselves into your nurturing hands.
Receive the devotions of our labors,
>the fruits of our vines,
>>and all that we are and know,
>>>that we may make a difference:
>>>>in our homes, in our communities,
>>>>and in our world.
Receive these sacrifices,
>as a pledge to live our beliefs,
>>through Jesus Christ,
>>>the pioneer and perfecter of our faith.

Invitation to Communion (Isaiah 5, Psalm 80, Hebrews 11)
Just as the sun shines on all who turn their faces to the light, just as the rain showers upon all who stand on open

ground, so God's grace in Christ comes as a blessing to all. Borne of the sweat of his suffering love, Christ willingly gave of himself, that we might be made free. You, who are willing to offer yourselves to God, come to the table in love and faith. Here we find forgiveness, hope, and the promise of eternal life.

SENDING FORTH

Benediction (Isaiah 5, Psalm 80, Hebrews 11)
Go forth into the world,
    singing a love-song in the vineyard of life.
Remember the Gardner who nurtures your faith
    and provides for your needs.
Grow into the promise of Christ,
    secure in the knowledge that you are loved.

CONTEMPORARY OPTIONS

Contemporary Gathering Words (Isaiah 5, Psalm 80, Hebrews 11)
Sing a song of praise for the vineyard of our beloved.
    Give us life, O Lord!
Clear your lives of the stones that hinder your growth.
    Give us life, O Lord!
Place your faith in the one who makes you strong.
    Give us life, O Lord!
Surrounded by that great cloud of witnesses,
call on the one who comes to save us.
    Give us life, O Lord!

Praise Sentences (Isaiah 5, Psalm 80, Hebrews 11)
Holy God, shine your light into our lives,
    and we will call upon your name!
Loving Christ, turn your face toward us,
    that we may be saved!
Holy Spirit, restore us in your grace,
    bless us with justice, and show us the way
to keep your vineyard from harm.

AUGUST 25, 2013

Fourteenth Sunday after Pentecost
Mary J. Scifres

COLOR
Green

SCRIPTURE READINGS
Jeremiah 1:4-10; Psalm 71:1-6; Hebrews 12:18-29; Luke 13:10-17

THEME IDEAS
The power of speech pulls together these disparate scripture readings. Jeremiah is afraid to speak because of his youthful inexperience. The psalmist cries out for God to lean down and listen to our pleas. Hebrews warns us of the impending doom for those who do not listen when God's servant speaks. And God's servant-child Jesus speaks and a woman is healed. Laying hands on her, Jesus faces the condemning words of the synagogue leader, and yet Jesus speaks out for the woman's right to be healed and freed from bondage, even on the Sabbath day. The power of speech is a mighty power indeed. As God speaks to and through us, we are empowered to transform the world into that unshakeable realm of love and justice.

INVITATION AND GATHERING

Call to Worship (Jeremiah 1, Hebrews 12)
Listen, servants of God,
for God speaks to us even now.

Speak, O Lord, for your servants are listening.
Hear, servants of God,
for God's words are all around us
for those who have ears to hear.
Open our ears, Holy One,
that we might hear and know your voice.
Perceive, servants of God,
for God's wisdom is planted within—
within our souls, within the words of scripture,
within the stories of our faith.
Our hearts are open, Spirit of Truth,
that we might hear as God speaks
and journey where Christ leads.

Opening Prayer (Jeremiah 1, Psalm 71, Luke 13)
Rock of Ages, God of Wisdom and Truth,
speak to us clearly,
that we might live in your wisdom
and walk in your truth.
As we open to your presence,
help us hear and receive your message this day.
Speak, that we might be healed and empowered.
On this Sabbath day,
we rejoice in your presence
and give thanks for the power of your Spirit,
speaking through our words
and living through our actions.
In your holy name, we pray. Amen.

PROCLAMATION AND RESPONSE

Prayer of Confession (Psalm 71)
God of refuge and strength,
cover us with your grace.
Uphold us with your strength,
and forgive us with your mercy.
As we confess our sins and admit our shortcomings,
rescue us from despair and self-condemnation,

that we may never feel separated from you
and your boundless love.
We confess these things
and the hidden burdens of our hearts.
(Silence may follow.)
Help us feel in our most inward parts,
that even as we have already been known,
so have we already been loved and forgiven.
For this we give you thanks and praise. Amen.

Words of Assurance (Psalm 71, Luke 13)
Christ is our hope as we trust in God and God's mercy.
Stand straight and tall, for your sins are forgiven!

Introduction to the Word (Jeremiah 1, Psalm 71)
Before we were formed, God knew us.
Before we could hear,
God whispered words of life in our souls.
As we reflect on this miraculous gift of presence,
may we listen for God's voice,
spoken in ancient times and speaking still,
calling us into a future of hope.

Response to the Word (Jeremiah 1, Psalm 71)
Hope in Yahweh, who is our Hope.
Trust in Christ, who is our Trust.
Live in the Spirit, who is our Life.
Listen and speak, as God has listened and spoken to us.

THANKSGIVING AND COMMUNION

Invitation to Offering (Jeremiah 1, Hebrews 12)
We have been called to speak and to live Christ's love in
the world. We do so by offering all that we have, all that
we are, and all that we do, trusting that God will use these
gifts to bring the unshakeable realm of love and justice to
our world.

Offering Prayer (Jeremiah 1, Hebrews 12, Luke 13)
We offer our thanks and joy this day,
as we return these offerings to you, O God.

Receive these gifts with our gratitude,
  as our true worship in reverence and awe
    for all that you have done,
    all that you have spoken,
    and all that you are doing still.

SENDING FORTH

Benediction (Jeremiah 1, Luke 13)
  Rejoice in God's presence.
  We rejoice in God's word.
  Live as Christ's people.
  We go now to speak of Christ's love.
  Celebrate healing in the Spirit.
  We will share the good news of God,
  in all that we say and in all that we do!

CONTEMPORARY OPTIONS

Contemporary Gathering Words (Jeremiah 1)
  Word of God, speak...
  for your servants are listening.
  Word of God, speak to us this day.
  Word of God, teach...
  for we yearn to grow in your likeness.
  Word of God, speak to us this day.
  Word of God, dwell in us...
  for we long to live as your people
  Word of God, speak to us this day.

Praise Sentences (Jeremiah 1, Psalm 71)
  Our God is a mighty God.
  Our God is a mighty God.
  Christ is our refuge and strength.
  Christ is our refuge and strength.
  God is speaking words of love and truth.
  God is speaking words of love and truth.

SEPTEMBER 1, 2013

Fifteenth Sunday after Pentecost

B. J. Beu

COLOR

Green

SCRIPTURE READINGS

Jeremiah 2:4-13; Psalm 81:1,10-16, Hebrews 13:1-8, 15-16; Luke 14:1, 7-14

THEME IDEAS

Today's scriptures are full of pathos from a God who wants only good things for God's people. Yet, time and again, we forsake living water for cracked cisterns that can hold no water. We defile the land that God has given us for our fulfillment. Our religious leaders do not know the laws of life, and our rulers transgress against the Lord. We seek the seats of honor rather than looking to the needs of others. How long will we neglect to show hospitality to strangers? How many times have we failed to see angels in our midst, who seek only to bless us? God's pathos flows from these passages. Will we listen? Will we hear? Will we honor the One who seeks our welfare?

INVITATION AND GATHERING

Call to Worship (Jeremiah 2, Psalm 81)
Sing aloud, people of God,
the Lord fills us with good things.

Shout for joy, children of the Holy One,
God feeds us with the finest wheat
and satisfies us with the sweetest honey.
Do not look to cracked cisterns to quench your thirst,
for our God is a fountain of living water,
a well overflowing with the water of life.
Sing aloud, people of God,
the Lord fills us with good things.

Opening Prayer (Jeremiah 2, Hebrews 13, Luke 14)

God of days ancient and new,
    speak to us your ancient words of wisdom.
Help us hear afresh
    Christ's message of love and servanthood.
Soften our hearts
    to sense your presence.
Open our eyes
    to see your guiding hand.
Open our ears
    to hear your call.
Change our lives
    to follow your path
        of justice and mercy.
In Christ's name, we pray. Amen.
(Mary J. Scifres)

—OR—

Opening Prayer or Response to the Word (Hebrews 13)

Teach us, God of abundant mercy,
    to treat others as we would have them treat us.
Help us show hospitality to strangers,
    for by doing so,
        many of us have entertained angels
            without knowing it.
Remind us to visit those who are imprisoned,
    as if we ourselves were in prison.
Give us the courage to speak out against torture,
    as if we ourselves were being tortured.

May we never neglect to do good,
or to share from our abundance,
for such sacrifices are pleasing in your sight.
In your holy name, we pray. Amen.

PROCLAMATION AND RESPONSE

Litany of Confession (Jeremiah 2, Psalm 81)

How long, O Lord, will you wait for us
to return to you in love and gratitude?
How long will you offer us bread
made from the finest wheat,
when we would rather fill our mouths
with dust and ash?
How long will you be for us living water,
when we are so enamored
with the cracked cisterns of our own making,
and the dry riverbeds
of our petty complaints?
How long will you stand by us,
when we exchange the glory we find in you
for vanity and things that do not profit?
How long, O Lord, will you wait
before we come to our senses?

Words of Assurance (Psalm 81:10, Hebrews 13:5)

God offers us these words and this hope:
"I am the LORD your God,
who brought you up out of the land of Egypt.
Open your mouth wide and I will fill it."
God offers us these words of assurance:
"I will never leave you or forsake you."
God is faithful, even when we are not.

Response to the Word (Psalm 81:13, Luke 14:11)

God beseeches us:
"O that my people would listen to me,
that Israel would walk in my ways!
Then I would quickly subdue their enemies,
and turn my hand against their foes."

Christ tells us:
"all who exalt themselves will be humbled,
and those who humble themselves
will be exalted."
Those who have ears to hear, take heed,
but also take heart,
for it is God's good pleasure
to give us the kingdom.

THANKSGIVING AND COMMUNION

Invitation to the Offering (Hebrews 13)
Hebrews reminds us to keep our lives free from the love
of money, to be content with what we have. In the freedom and contentment that comes from abiding in Christ,
let us return thanks to God for our many blessings as we
collect today's offering.

Offering Prayer (Jeremiah 2, Psalm 81, Luke 14)
From slavery to our self-interest, O God,
you have freed us.
From starvation in the wilderness
of our self-exaltation,
you have brought us into a land
of choicest wheat and sweetest honey.
As we return a portion of the gifts you have given us,
remind us anew that the banquet of your love
is open to all people—
especially the poor, the crippled, the lame,
the blind, and all those who suffer.
May these gifts bring healing and light
into a world burdened by anguish and despair.
Amen.

SENDING FORTH

Benediction (Hebrews 13)
Let mutual love continue,
and we will find peace.

Let mutual love flourish,
and we will see God.
Let mutual love grow,
and we will never find ourselves forsaken.
Let mutual love abide,
and we will never be alone.
Thanks be to God!

CONTEMPORARY OPTIONS

Contemporary Gathering Words (Psalm 81)
Sing to God.
Sing God's praises.
Eat your fill of food that truly satisfies.
God gives us the choicest breads
and the sweetest honey.
Swim in the waters of life.
Laugh and splash and play
in the wellspring of God's salvation.
Sing to God.
Sing God's praises.

Praise Sentences (Psalm 81)
Sing aloud to God.
Shout for joy to the God who loves us.
Sing aloud to God
Shout for joy to the God who loves us.

SEPTEMBER 8, 2013

Sixteenth Sunday after Pentecost
Deborah Sokolove

COLOR
Green

SCRIPTURE READINGS
Jeremiah 18:1-11; Psalm 139:1-6, 13-18; Philemon 1-21; Luke 14:25-33

THEME IDEAS
God knows our intentions and our hopes, reshaping us when we do what is wrong, and responding to our repentance with mercy. We count the cost of our actions, but Jesus calls us to let go of our attachments and follow him in a life of love and care for others. This mystery is beyond our understanding.

INVITATION AND GATHERING

Call to Worship (Jeremiah 18, Psalm 139)
We come with praise
for the wonderful works of God.
> **Even before we speak,**
> **God knows us completely.**
The Holy One knows us and sustains us,
even in our moments of confusion and doubt.
> **Who can count the thoughts of God?**

They are more than all the sands of the desert.
Like clay in the hand of the potter,
we are shaped into vessels of divine will.
We come with praise
for the wonderful works of God.

Opening Prayer (Jeremiah 18, Psalm 139)
Boundless Shaper of people and nations,
you are beyond our knowing,
yet closer to us than our every breath.
You are before us and behind us,
surrounding us with your love,
and fashioning all of creation
in the secret depths of your heart.
With every thought, with every song,
and with every prayer,
turn these fragile, earthen vessels of our lives,
into the Spirit-filled body of Christ. Amen.

PROCLAMATION AND RESPONSE

Prayer of Confession (Psalm 139, Philemon, Luke 14)
God of our lives,
you search us and know us.
We have refused to take up your cross,
to bear the burdens that are ours to carry.
We have not given up our attachments
to possessions or to self.
We have not counted the cost
of walking into an unknown future with you.
Help us turn away from evil,
that we may walk with you once more.

Words of Assurance (Psalm 139)
The Holy One rejoices in our repentance,
reshaping us into vessels of love and service.
In the grace-filled love of Christ, we are forgiven.
Thanks be to God. Amen.

Passing the Peace of Christ (Philemon)

Grace to you, and peace from God, the Mother and Father
of our Lord Jesus Christ.
The peace of Christ be with you.
The peace of Christ be also with you.

Prayer of Preparation (Jeremiah 18, Psalm 139)

Holy Shaper of hearts and minds,
    as Jeremiah came to know you
        in the work of the potter's hands,
            teach us your ways
                in the reading of your word.
Lead us into a deeper understanding of your ways,
    that we may know and do your will. Amen.

Response to the Word (Luke 14)

Holy Shaper of life and grace,
    you have shown us the cost of being your people.
We give you thanks, for the crosses
    that are ours to bear,
        and for the strength to carry them.
Help us follow the path of Jesus,
    who shows us the way. Amen.

THANKSGIVING AND COMMUNION

Offering Prayer (Luke 14)

With these gifts,
    we lay down all that we have
        and all that we are,
            and take up the cross with Jesus.

—OR—

Offering Prayer (Jeremiah 18, Philemon)

Generous and loving God,
    we thank you for the many joys
        and signs of encouragement in our lives.
With these gifts,
    create signs of encouragement and joy

in the lives of others,
    and in the ministries of our church.
In Christ's name, we pray. Amen.
(Mary Scifres)

Invitation to Communion (Psalm 139, Luke 14)

The bread is ready, the cup is filled,
    the table is set.
Let all who are hungry for the love of God,
    come and be fed.
Let all who are thirsty for new life,
    come and share the cup.
Let all who want to follow Jesus,
    come and join the feast.

SENDING FORTH

Benediction (Luke 14)

With empty hands and open hearts,
    go forth to follow Jesus
    in love and service to the world.

CONTEMPORARY OPTIONS

Contemporary Gathering Words (Luke 14)

We come to take up the cross that is laid before us.
We come with praise for the wonderful works of God.

—OR—

Contemporary Gathering Words (Jeremiah 18, Luke 14)

Come to Christ, who calls us by name.
    We walk on the path of the cross.
Come to God, who shapes our lives.
    We walk on the path of the cross.
Come to the Spirit, who molds our hearts.
    We walk on the path of the cross.
(Mary Scifres)

Praise Sentences (Psalm 139)
  How weighty are your thoughts, O God!
  How vast is the sum of them!
  They are more than the sand.
  We come to the end and there is only you.

SEPTEMBER 15, 2013

Seventeenth Sunday after Pentecost
Karin Ellis

COLOR
Green

SCRIPTURE READINGS
Jeremiah 4:11-12, 22-28; Psalm 14:1-7; 1 Timothy 1:12-17; Luke 15:1-10

THEME IDEAS
Humanity's evil and foolish ways unite these scriptures. Likening God's people to stupid children who have no understanding, Jeremiah proclaims that God will visit ruin and devastation upon the very earth to shake us to our core. The psalmist laments that while fools say in their hearts: "There is no God," God looks for the wise of heart but finds none—for all have gone astray. Even so, the psalmist waits for the day when the Lord will restore the fortunes of Israel. Paul rejoices that he has received mercy through Christ, though he was formerly a blasphemer and a man of violence against the church. And while the scribes and Pharisees grumble that Jesus eats with tax collectors and sinners, Jesus reminds them that there is more joy in heaven over a sinner who repents than over ninety-nine righteous persons who need no repentance. Human beings are prone to evil and foolishness, but we worship

a God who seeks the lost and rejoices when the lost are found. (B. J. Beu)

INVITATION AND GATHERING

Call to Worship (Psalm 14, 1 Timothy 1)
Fools say in their hearts, "There is no God."
We proclaim that God's presence is real
and alive and thriving!
Evildoers declare through their actions,
"We go through life alone."
But we see God's grace, faithfulness,
and steadfast love in our lives
and in the world around us.
Praise be to God!

—OR—

Call to Worship (Psalm 14, 1 Timothy 1)
Rejoice, O daughters of Zion!
Sing praise, O sons of Israel!
For in Christ, we are children of God.
In Christ, hope is born again!
Rejoice, O daughters of Zion!
Sing praise, O sons of Israel!
For in Christ, we find refuge and strength.
In Christ, love is born again!
(Mary Scifres and B. J. Beu)

Opening Prayer (Jeremiah 4, Luke 15)
God of abundant grace,
may your Holy Spirit be with us now
as we worship you this day.
Open our eyes to truly see one another,
that we might discover your presence
in the smile of a neighbor.
Open our ears to the needs of the world,
that we might hear your wisdom
in the words spoken around us.

And open our hearts to your grace and love,
    that we might find guidance
        and strength for the journey,
            for ourselves and for one another. Amen.

—OR—

Opening Prayer (Psalm 14, Luke 15)

O God of heaven and earth,
    look upon us now
        with mercy and grace.
Enter our hearts
    and make us holy.
Be our Shepherd,
    and guide us in your ways,
        that we may no longer wander alone.
Hear our cries,
    and gather us to yourself,
        that we may be one with each other
            through the power of your Holy Spirit.
Amen.
(Mary Scifres and B. J. Beu)

PROCLAMATION AND RESPONSE

Prayer of Confession (Jeremiah 4, 1 Timothy 1)

Gracious and loving God,
    we find it difficult at times
        to place our trust in you.
Too often we look at the world,
    and see only violence, pain, destruction,
        and signs of hopelessness and despair.
Too often we rely on our own strength,
    our own plans, our own devices,
        rather than trusting in your hand to hold us,
            your love to sustain us,
                and your wisdom to see us through.
Forgive us, Holy One.

Help us turn to you when we are lost,
　　that we might find our way home.
Help us navigate the treacherous waters of this world,
　　that we might experience your abundant grace,
　　　mercy, and love.
Help us put our trust in you,
　　that the faith and love that are in Christ Jesus
　　　may shine in our lives for all to see. Amen.

Words of Assurance (Luke 15:7)

Jesus said, "there will be more joy in heaven
　　over one sinner who repents than over ninety-nine
　　righteous persons who need no repentance."
My friends, experience God's forgiveness and joy—
　　gifts that leads to new life!

Passing the Peace of Christ (1 Timothy 1)

Like a waterfall that descends down the mountain, open
your hearts to receive God's faith and love, as they flow
into our lives through Jesus the Christ. Turn and share this
abundance with one another!

Introduction to the Word (1 Timothy 1)

May the words that are spoken,
　　and the reflections of our hearts,
　　　be worthy of your grace, O God,
　　　　to whom all honor and glory is given
　　　　　now and forever more. Amen.

Response to the Word (Jeremiah 4, Luke 15)

God of love and mercy,
　　may the truth you offer
　　　stay with us when we leave this place;
　　may all that is lost in our lives,
　　　be found through your Spirit;
　　may the brokenness of this world
　　　be healed and turned to love and hope;
　　and may we strive to be your faithful disciples
　　　as the body of Christ. Amen.

THANKSGIVING AND COMMUNION

Invitation to the Offering (1 Timothy 1)

Brothers and sisters in Christ, we have received much
from God—grace, mercy, abundance, the love of Christ,
and the gift of life itself. In our worship, we praise God
and give God thanks for these gifts. Let us now offer what
we can as a way of saying, "Thank you." In gratitude for
God's generosity, let us share God's abundance with one
another.

Offering Prayer (1 Timothy 1)

Gracious and loving God,
> we thank you for these gifts
> > and ask that they be used
> > > to help the needy in our community
> > > and throughout the world.
As we offer you these gifts,
> we offer ourselves as well,
> > that together we might transform the world
> > > with your grace and love. Amen.

SENDING FORTH

Benediction (Luke 15)

My friends, go into the world:
> knowing that it is God who loves us,
> Christ who strengthens us,
> and the Holy Spirit who empowers us for service.
Go in peace and joy! Amen.

Benediction (1 Timothy 1, Luke 15)

Christ has welcomed us here.
> **The Spirit sends us forth.**
God has called us to serve.
> **Christ has shown us how.**
The Spirit has made us whole.
> **Love sends us forth!**
(Mary Scifres and B. J. Beu)

CONTEMPORARY OPTIONS

Contemporary Gathering Words (Luke 15)

When the lost are found,
there is joy!
When hope overcomes despair,
there is joy!
When we seek and find God's faithfulness,
there is joy!

Praise Sentences (1 Timothy 1)

Praise to God who is present to us
through Christ Jesus!
Praise to God who is present to us
through one another!

Praise Sentences (Psalm 47, 1 Timothy 1)

Rejoice in the Lord.
Rejoice and be glad!
Rejoice in the Lord.
Rejoice and be glad!
Rejoice in the Lord.
Rejoice and be glad,
now and forevermore!
(Mary Scifres and B. J. Beu)

SEPTEMBER 22, 2013

Eighteenth Sunday after Pentecost
B. J. Beu

COLOR
Green

SCRIPTURE READINGS
Jeremiah 8:18–9:1; Psalm 79:1-9; 1 Timothy 2:1-7; Luke 16:1-13

THEME IDEAS
Stewardship is a natural way to focus these readings. While Jeremiah and the psalmist cry out to God for help in the midst of Israel's distress, there is much that bodies of faith can do to ease one another's suffering. In Luke, Jesus tells the perplexing parable about the dishonest steward who, after being fired for mismanaging his master's accounts, acts shrewdly to ingratiate himself to those who owe his master money. Jesus challenges the children of light to be as wise with their generation as was this dishonest steward. Proper management of our time, talents, and treasure matters, for if we cannot be trusted to be good stewards of dishonest wealth, how can God trust us to be faithful stewards of true riches?

INVITATION AND GATHERING
Call to Worship (Jeremiah 8, Psalm 79)
Call upon the Lord, for God hears our pleas.
Cry a river of tears to wash away life's sorrow.

Put your faith in God, our great physician.
Reach out for the balm of Gilead,
for God hears the cries of the suffering.
The Lord delivers the faithful
to the glory of God's name.
We will call upon the Lord,
for God hears our pleas.
Enter God's gates with hope and gladness.

Opening Prayer (Jeremiah 8:21-22, Psalm 79:8-9)
Righteous God,
let your compassion come speedily to meet us,
for we are brought low in our need.
Our spirits are poured out like flowing waters,
and there is no one to aid us in our pain.
Can you not hear the scoffers say,
"Is there no balm in Gilead?
Is there no physician there?"
Help us, O God of our salvation,
for the glory of your name.
Let your compassion come speedily to us once more,
that all may see and know
where true help lies. Amen.

PROCLAMATION AND RESPONSE

Prayer of Confession (Jeremiah 8, Psalm 79, Luke 16)
We hear your calling to be faithful stewards, O God,
but find your road a hard one to walk.
We cannot seem to be good stewards,
even of dishonest wealth,
much less the riches of your spiritual gifts.
Forgive us when we try to serve two masters—
we love you and want your blessings,
but we place our trust in human wealth,
status, and power.
Forgive our hesitation
to take the medicine you prescribe,

for you are our one true physician,
  healing the brokenness
    of our self-centered ways. Amen.

Assurance of Pardon (Jeremiah 8, 1 Timothy 2)
The One who weeps for us and for our world,
  the One who is the author of our salvation,
  is the God of compassion—
    the One who meets us in our need
    and forgives our failings. Amen.

Response to the Word (1 Timothy 2:4)
Take heart, people of God,
  for the Holy One desires everyone to be saved
  and to come to know the truth.
Put your faith in Christ,
  the mediator between heaven and earth,
  and you will live.

THANKSGIVING AND COMMUNION

Offering Prayer (Luke 16)
Precious Lord,
  you provide for our every need,
    and call us to be good stewards
    of your many gifts.
May we be found faithful in a little,
  that we may also be faithful in a lot.
In loving gratitude,
  we offer you these gifts
    as a sign of our desire
      to live as children of light—
        children of your healing love.
In Jesus' name we pray. Amen.

SENDING FORTH

Benediction (Luke 16)
Be faithful with a little,
  that you may be faithful with much.

Be faithful with much,
    that you may be entrusted
    with the wealth and welfare of others.
Be faithful with the wealth of this generation,
    that you may be given true riches.
Be faithful as children of light
    and serve only one master,
    that you may know the grace, hope, and peace
    of the One who is truly faithful.

CONTEMPORARY OPTIONS

Contemporary Gathering Words (Jeremiah 8, Psalm 79)

Worship God, who hears our pleas.
**Worship God, who replaces our tears of sorrow
with tears of joy.**
Worship God, who is our one true physician.
Worship God, who heals the sin-sick soul.
Worship God, you peoples.
We will worship the Lord our God.

Praise Sentences (1 Timothy)

Christ is merciful.
Thanks be to God!
Christ is mediator of heaven and earth.
Thanks be to God!
Christ offers us eternal life.
Thanks be to God!

SEPTEMBER 29, 2013

Nineteenth Sunday after Pentecost
Amy B. Hunter

COLOR
Green

SCRIPTURE READINGS
Jeremiah 32:1-3a, 6-15; Psalm 91:1-6, 14-16; 1 Timothy 6:6-19; Luke 16:19-31

THEME IDEAS
We can trust God in all circumstances and with all aspects of our lives. In the midst of enemy occupation and on the brink of exile, the prophet Jeremiah trusts that God has a promising future for the Hebrew people and their homeland. A seemingly irrational act in enemy-occupied territory, Jeremiah buys the deed to a piece of property as a statement of radical trust in God. Psalm 91 is a litany of trust in the face of dangers—a trust answered by God's own words of reassurance. Timothy reminds us that even in settled times, wealth and status, rather than war and physical danger, often lure us away from placing our faith in God. Luke emphasizes this point through the caricature of a rich man who does not trust God. The unnamed rich man is so wrapped up in his status and wealth that even in the torment of death, he still is trying to take charge of his life and of God. Trusting in God, we find the

peace that passes all understanding and the strength to heed Christ's call.

INVITATION AND GATHERING

Call to Worship (Psalm 91)
Those who love God,
God will deliver.
Those who know God by name,
God will protect.
Those who call out to God,
God will answer.
We gather this morning,
as those who trust God.

Opening Prayer (1 Timothy 6)
O Gentle One, we pray for your presence
among us this day.
Where there is fear, let us know your comfort.
Where there is doubt, let us know your confidence.
Where there is joy, let us know your pleasure.
Where there is regret, let us know your forgiveness.
Where there is pain, let us know your compassion.
Fill this place with your Holy Spirit,
and may this same Spirit fill our lives in this time
of worship, and in the week ahead. Amen.
(Mary J. Scifres)

—OR—

Opening Prayer or Prayer of the People (Jeremiah 32, Psalm 91, 1 Timothy 6)
Almighty God,
you create, redeem and sustain us,
every moment of our lives.
In you we place our trust.
When we face illness, conflict, and fear,
you are our steadfast protector.
When we suffer setback and loss,
you restore us through your love.

When our lives prosper and we are comfortable,
  you move us to share our blessings with others.
In times of hardship and plenty,
  you alone are the source of the life
    that really is life.
Holy God,
  in love and trust,
    we live the power of your resurrection,
      through Jesus Christ, our Lord. Amen.

PROCLAMATION AND RESPONSE

Prayer of Confession (Jeremiah 32, Psalm 91, 1 Timothy 6, Luke 16)
  Triune God,
    you call us to trust you
      in every circumstance of our lives,
        yet far too often,
          we do not.
In times of oppression and strife,
  we lose hope in our future.
When enduring natural disasters,
  suffering illness, or facing death,
    we often grow bitter and forget your love.
Stripped of the idols of our wealth and status,
  we try in vain to control our lives.
Eager to be powerful and successful,
  we wander away from you,
    falling into the pain of addiction, greed,
      and blind ambition.
Absorbed by our wants and desires,
  we are blind to those around us who need our care.
Forgive us, O God.
Forgive our despair, our bitterness, and our fear.
Turn our hearts to you,
  that we may taste fullness of life
    and trust your promised salvation.

Words of Assurance (Psalm 91)

God's loving presence never abandons us,
 not even when we abandon God.
God delivers those who seek and love the Lord.
All we have to do is call, and God answers us.
God answers us with rescue and honor,
 forgiveness and mercy, life and salvation.

Passing the Peace of Christ

We call out to God and God answers us. Invited into the shelter of the Most High, we rejoice and greet one another with the peace of Jesus Christ.

Introduction to the Word (Jeremiah 32:6)

God, help us to say with Jeremiah,
"The word of the LORD came to me."
I know this is the word of the Lord.

Response to the Word (Jeremiah 32, Psalm 91, 1 Timothy 6, Luke 16)

God, your holy word invites us to place our trust in you.
May the words we have heard here today,
 take root in our lives.
May the words we have received in our hearts,
 strengthen us to live more boldly in faith,
 that we may trust you in disaster and boon,
 in good times and bad, in death and in life.
"The word of the LORD came to me."
I know this is the word of the Lord.

THANKSGIVING AND COMMUNION

Invitation to the Offering (1 Timothy 6)

Wealth, status, and success are uncertain, but we can trust God's abundant provision, and God's desire that we enjoy what we have. Let us respond by working for justice, living generously, and sharing with others.

Offering Prayer (1 Timothy 6)

Beloved God,
   who richly provides for our needs and enjoyment,
      thank you for your many gifts.
You have trusted us with our lives, with this world,
   and with your love.
May the gifts we offer you today
   be used for your service and your glory.
Help us store up for ourselves
   the treasure of a good foundation for the future,
      that we may take hold of the life
         that really is life.
We offer these gifts,
   trusting in our savior Jesus Christ. Amen.

SENDING FORTH

Benediction (Psalm 91, 1 Timothy 6)

Pursue righteousness, godliness,
faith, love, endurance, and gentleness.
Live boldly, trusting God with everything you are
and everything you have.
Take hold of the life to which God calls you.
Go forth, rejoicing in God.
   Thanks be to God!

CONTEMPORARY OPTIONS

Contemporary Gathering Words (Psalm 91)

Come and worship the Most High,
our shelter from the storm.
   We will trust our God!
God delivers us from temptations and troubles.
   We will trust our God!
God heals us when disease and disaster strike.
   We will trust our God!
God protects those who call out for help.
   We will trust our God!

God offers us eternal life and shows us our salvation.
We will trust our God!

Praise Sentences (1 Timothy 6)
We trust our God,
who alone gives us life.
We trust our God,
who gives us life in Jesus Christ.
We trust our God,
who gives us life in the Spirit.
Give blessing and praise to our God,
who alone deserves every honor!

OCTOBER 6, 2013

Twentieth Sunday after Pentecost /
World Communion Sunday

B. J. Beu

COLOR
Green or White

SCRIPTURE READINGS
Lamentations 1:1-6; Psalm 137; 2 Timothy 1:1-14; Luke 17:5-10

THEME IDEAS
These readings stand as a warning to those who believe that faith ensures prosperity. For certainly not everyone in Judah forsook the Lord when Babylon and the surrounding nations destroyed the holy city of Jerusalem and sent her people into exile. Lamentations and Psalm 137 speak of tears, groans, distress, and unremitting suffering for a people used to fine pastures and the joys of God's delight. Second Timothy makes clear that Paul's suffering is a result of preaching the gospel of Jesus Christ, the gospel of power and grace. Sharing the truth is its own reward. Finally, Christ warns his disciples that those who labor in the fields are not invited to come in and dine when their work is done. No, they must first go to prepare the meal for their master. Working for the gospel is its own reward, and those who do so should not expect

special dispensations of earthly ease and comfort. But when we guard the good treasure entrusted to us, rather than seeking to protect earthly comforts, the Holy Spirit helps us in our time of need.

INVITATION AND GATHERING

Call to Worship (Lamentations 1, Psalm 137, 2 Timothy 2)
When we feel like stags without pasture,
where can we turn for help?
We look to God for grace.
When our friends cannot comfort us in our distress,
where can we turn for solace?
We look to Christ for mercy.
When our adversaries rejoice at our misfortune,
where can we turn for the strength to carry on?
We look to the Holy Spirit for peace.
Put your trust in God, our guide and guardian.
We worship the One who leads us back to life.

Opening Prayer (Lamentations 1, Psalm 137, 2 Timothy 2)
Merciful God,
when grief threatens to overwhelm us
and our mouths know the taste of bitter tears,
call us back to the land of the living;
when adversaries rejoice over our misfortune,
and ask us for songs of our former glory,
bless us with hope and a sincere faith;
when fear fills us with a spirit of cowardice,
and our courage flees like a deer before its prey,
give us a spirit of power and love
and of self-discipline,
that we may be brought back to life,
through the grace of the one
who abolished death. Amen.

PROCLAMATION AND RESPONSE

Prayer of Confession (2 Timothy 1, Luke 17)

Holy One,
    we cringe when we hear Paul's invitation
        to join him in suffering for the gospel—
            for we would prefer not to suffer at all
            if we can help it;
    we resist Paul's instruction
        to rely on your power and grace to save us—
            for we would rather trust our own efforts,
                our own resources,
                    and our own cleverness,
                        than really step out in faith;
    we turn a deaf ear to Paul's confession
        that he is not ashamed of the gospel—
            for we would rather not look foolish
                in the eyes of others.
We are ashamed of our cowardice, Holy One.
Give us the courage to follow you anew,
    for you do not give a spirit of cowardice,
        but a spirit of power and love. Amen.

Words of Assurance (2 Timothy 1)

God has given us a spirit of power and of love
    and of self-discipline.
The Spirit has given us treasure from heaven
    to strengthen us on our way.
Christ has given us the gospel of truth,
    that we might live.
The One who gives us these gifts and more,
    forgives our faults
    and offers us bread for the journey
    and wine to gladden the heart.
Rejoice in the mercy of our God.

Passing the Peace of Christ (2 Timothy 1)

Our fellowship is filled with grandmothers like Lois and
mothers like Eunice, who nurture us in our faith. Our

fellowship is filled with teachers like Paul, who yearn to share the gospel. Our fellowship is filled with students like Timothy, who want to know the hope to which they have been called. See these people in the faces around you, as you pass the peace of Christ.

Response to the Word (2 Timothy 1:13-14)

Hold fast to the teaching you have received.
Hold true to the faith and love
    that are ours in Christ Jesus.
Guard the treasure of new life in Christ,
    through the help of the Spirit living within you.

THANKSGIVING AND COMMUNION

Offering Prayer (Psalm 137)

Even in a strange land among people with foreign ways,
    you invite us to sit along the riverbank, O God,
        and bloom where we are planted.
Even when our hearts are heavy,
    and the spirit within us cries out in anguish,
        you invite us to take up instruments
            and sing songs of joyful memory.
You are the One who never leaves us,
    O God of tender mercy.
You alone can turn our tears of sadness
    into tears of joy.
Use these offerings to turn shouts of despair
    into shouts of mirth and gladness.
Bless these offerings,
    that the world may know
        that you have the power
            to bring the dead back to life.

Communion Litany (World Communion Sunday)

Once we were not a people.
Now we are God's people.
Once we had no place to call our home.
Now we abide in the everlasting arms.

Once we had no family.
Now all those who confess Jesus with their lips,
and do the works of Christian love,
are our sisters and brothers.
Once we ate but were never satisfied.
Now we feast on the living bread,
the bread of heaven.
Once we drank, but our thirst was never quenched.
Now we drink our fill from God's cup,
the cup of blessing.
Once we were not a people.
Now we belong to Christ.

SENDING FORTH

Benediction (World Communion Sunday)
With Christians around the world,
we are united as Christ's body,
in a world torn apart by division and isolation.
Knit together in Christian love,
we leave here to share living bread
with a world starving for spiritual food.
With Christians around the world,
we are blessed through fellowship with Christ,
in union with God and the Holy Spirit.
Woven together in Christian hope,
we leave here to share the cup of salvation
with a world dying of thirst.

CONTEMPORARY OPTIONS

Contemporary Gathering Words (World Communion Sunday)
In Jesus, all Christians are one body.
But we feel isolated from one another,
separated by customs and beliefs.
In Jesus, all Christians are one body.
But we don't worship alike.

Besides, we speak different languages.
In Jesus, all Christians are one body.
Come share the Lord!

Praise Sentences (World Communion Sunday)

Praise God who gives us the bread of life.
Praise Christ who unites in the breaking of the bread.
Praise Christ who binds us together in the common cup.
Praise the Spirit who makes us one.

OCTOBER 13, 2013

Twenty-first Sunday after Pentecost
Mary J. Scifres

COLOR

Green

SCRIPTURE READINGS

Jeremiah 29:1, 4-7; Psalm 66:1-12; 2 Timothy 2:8-15; Luke 17:11-19

THEME IDEAS

Although "bloom where you are planted" never appears in scripture, today's readings point to just this message. Through Jeremiah, God reminds the exiled Israelites that they are to live fully and caringly in Babylon. They are even to pray for the welfare of the city to which they have been exiled. The psalmist praises God for mighty deeds, even while remembering the burdens and troublesome journeys of their lives. Paul reminds Timothy to endure as Christ endures, as Paul himself is enduring, in order to remain faithful, following Christ and answering God's call. Jesus heals ten people with skin diseases on the journey between Samaria and Galilee, then sends them on their way. To the one who returns with gratitude, Jesus offers a further blessing of faith and wholeness. As followers of Christ, as God's people, we are a people on a journey. Wherever that journey takes us, we are called to build and to grow, to share ministry and to serve, to praise

and to worship, to live and to endure whatever circumstances we are given.

INVITATION AND GATHERING

Call to Worship (Psalm 66, Luke 17)
Sing loud and long. Make noises of joy.
Sing glory to God on high!
Remembering burdens of trouble,
and journeys of sorrow,
we come in prayer and praise.
Listening to Christ's call to faith and hope,
we answer with lives of service and love.
Let us worship in gratitude and praise this day.

Opening Prayer (Jeremiah 29, Luke 17)
Journeyman, Gardener, Builder, and Giver of Life,
plant your seeds of hope and faith within us.
Help us be a people of light and love,
that others might see your power in our lives.
Touch us with your holy presence,
and your healing strength,
that we might move forward in faith
and our lives might be fulfilled.
In gratitude and joy, we pray. Amen.

PROCLAMATION AND RESPONSE

Prayer of Confession (Jeremiah 29, Psalm 66, Luke 17)
Awesome God,
have mercy on us.
Guide us through the fires of temptation,
and save us from the floods of selfishness.
Lift us from the burden of despair—
despair that would prevent us
from walking forth as your people
and answering your call.
Heal us, O Jesus,
as you healed the lepers of old.

Forgive us, O God,
   and plant your seeds of forgiveness
     in our lives and in our church,
     that we might forgive,
       even as we are forgiven.
Build us into your body of Christ,
   in this time and place. Amen.

Words of Assurance (Jeremiah 29, Luke 17)
Build houses and live in them.
Plant gardens and eat your fill.
God is with us even in our most distant journeys.
Christ can heal us, even in our deepest despair.
Get up and go on your way.
Your faith has made you well!

Passing the Peace of Christ (Jeremiah 29)
Seek the welfare of this place and its people. Share signs of love and peace, as you greet and pray for your neighbor this day. In this we flower as God's people.

Introduction to the Word (2 Timothy 2)
Paul reminds Timothy that the word of God is not chained. In speaking God's truth, we are proclaiming grace that frees, and love that heals. Listen, as the promises of God are spoken and proclaimed, freely and joyously this day.

Response to the Word (Jeremiah 29, Psalm 66, Luke 17)
Be with us on this journey of life, O God.
Walk beside us and support us,
   when we are burdened and sinking low.
Talk to us and guide us,
   when we are lost and unsure.
Live in us and work through us,
   when others are in need of your presence.
Free us from the pit of despair,
   and bless us with your healing touch,
     that we may go forth in faith and hope
       to sing your praises,

even as we answer your call
to love and to serve one another.
In Christ's name, we pray.

THANKSGIVING AND COMMUNION

Invitation to the Offering (Jeremiah 29)
"Bloom where you are planted," an old saying goes. "Seek
the welfare of the city where I have sent you," God says
through Jeremiah. As the people planted in this church at
this time, let us give generously, that the love of God may
be planted in others, through the ministry and mission of
this church.

Offering Prayer (Psalm 66, Luke 17)
Amazing, mighty God,
we have seen your awesome deeds
in our lives and in our world.
We give thanks for the miraculous ways
you love and heal us.
Work through these gifts we now return to you,
that our lives and ministries
may be instruments of healing and hope,
and signs of love and life.
In gratitude and joy, we pray. Amen.

SENDING FORTH

Benediction (Luke 17)
Get up, get out of here!
**We're going! We're going now,
to follow where Christ leads.**
Go in faith—faith that has made you well.
**We're going! We're going, with hope and love,
that others may find wellness and faith in God.**

—OR—

Benediction (Jeremiah 29, Luke 17)
Bloom where you are planted.
Grow seeds of faith and hope.

We are seeds of God's own love.
Care for your neighbors.
Live with kindness and compassion.
We are seeds of God's own love.
Live in Christ. Love as Christ loves.
Heal with Christ's powerful mercy.
We are seeds of God's own love.

CONTEMPORARY OPTIONS

Contemporary Gathering Words (Jeremiah 29)
Have you wandered far from God?
Are you stuck in despair?
Build houses of hope.
Plant gardens of faith.
Offer prayers of love.
For even in the farthest reaches of our journey,
God is with us.
God is with us.
God is with us.
God is with us.
God is with us even now.

Praise Sentences (Psalm 66)
Sing glory to God. Worship Christ's name!
Sing glory to God. Worship Christ's name!

Praise Sentences (Psalm 66)
Sing praise to God. Let your praises be heard.
Sing praise to God. Let your praises be heard.
Make a joyful noise this day.
Make a joyful noise this day.

OCTOBER 20, 2013

Twenty-second Sunday after Pentecost
Peter Bankson

COLOR
Green

SCRIPTURE READINGS
Jeremiah 31:27-34; Psalm 119:97-104; 2 Timothy 3:14–4:5; Luke 18:1-8

THEME IDEAS
The days are surely coming when God will make a new covenant with people of faith. This new covenant is being written on the hearts of God's people. God will write the law upon our hearts and stay with us. As this occurs, we will know God's truth and no longer need to be taught. Even so, while God's truth is beyond words, the words of scripture are useful for teaching, guiding our lives, and training in righteousness. Keep praying, keep witnessing, keep sharing God's good news, for living in God's word helps us stay on track. When all else fails, look around— the heavens and the earth show us the creativity of God. Finally, be persistent. God will bring justice, even though people don't seem to care.

INVITATION AND GATHERING

Call to Worship (Jeremiah 31, Psalm 119)
Come, people of God.
Come together in the presence of our Creator.

We come, hungry for the new covenant
God promises to write on our hearts.
Come, people of faith.
God is here to fill us with wisdom and patience.
We come, yearning for God's justice
and faithful presence in our world.

Opening Prayer (Jeremiah 31, 2 Timothy 3–4) \|25\|15
Holy God of all creation,
  we gather once again
    to celebrate our commitment
      to be your church in this time and place.
As the prophet Jeremiah reminds us,
  the days are surely coming,
    when you will make a new covenant with us:
      you will be our God
        and we shall be your people.
God of the open future,
  write your law within our hearts this morning,
    and in the days to come,
      that we may be a people
        committed to the way of Christ,
          who is our Savior. Amen.

PROCLAMATION AND RESPONSE

Prayer of Confession (Psalm 119, 2 Timothy 3–4)
O Patient, Forgiving Fountain of Justice,
  your words are sweet,
    holding us back from evil ways.
Yet even when we know your will for our lives,
we find ourselves distracted by our desires,
ever turning away from your truth
to wander paths that lead us astray.
You offer us a better future and a new relationship,
  where you will plant your truth within us,
    equipping us for every good work,
      and yet, we're still so easily distracted.

Holy God,
   give us the wisdom to see ourselves
     as we really are;
   grant us the courage
     to confess our failure to keep your word.

Words of Assurance (Jeremiah 31:33b-34)
   God has promised us a new covenant declaring:
     "I will put my law within you,
     and I will write it on your hearts,
     and I will be your God and you shall be my people.
     I will forgive your iniquity,
     and remember your sin no more."
   Thanks be to God, we are forgiven.

Passing the Peace of Christ (Jeremiah 31)
   We celebrate the presence of the risen Christ, the one who
   shows us how to claim God's new covenant of love.
   The peace of Christ be with you always.
   The peace of Christ be with you always.

Prayer of Preparation (Psalm 119)
   Let the words of my mouth
     and the meditation of my heart
       be acceptable to you, O Lord,
         my rock and my redeemer.

Response to the Word (Jeremiah 31, Psalm 119,
2 Timothy 3–4)
   God of all that was and is and that shall be,
     open our hearts to receive your wisdom.
   Help us know how to share the good news
     you are writing on our hearts. Amen.

THANKSGIVING AND COMMUNION

Invitation to the Offering (Luke 18)
   The law of God is being written on our hearts,
     opening us to the needs of others.
   Let us share what we've been given with those in need.

Offering Prayer (Jeremiah 31, 2 Timothy 3–4)
Holy God, Inspiring Wellspring of Compassion,
   we come to you, offering our lives and our industry,
      as fruit of the good news you are bringing
         into the world.
Bless these gifts,
   that others may be touched
      by the grace and tender mercy
         we have found in your love. Amen.

Invitation to Communion (Jeremiah 31, Psalm 119, 2 Timothy 3–4)
Holy God,
   we thank you for the new covenant
      you are writing upon our hearts.
Loving Christ,
   we celebrate the opportunity
      to share your good news
         with our sisters and brothers in faith.
Empowering Holy Spirit,
   we give you thanks
      for your strength and encouragement
         to persevere when the road is hard.
Merciful God,
   fill us with the bread of life
      and the wine of gladness,
         as we gather to share your presence
            in the bread and cup. Amen.

SENDING FORTH

Benediction (Jeremiah 31, Psalm 119, 2 Timothy 3–4, Luke 18)
As we go forth to share the good news
of God's emerging covenant, remember this:
   The law of God is being written on our hearts.
Keep praying, keep witnessing,
keep sharing God's good news,

for God brings justice to our world,
even when we don't seem to care.
God is bringing justice even now,
when we live as Christ's disciples
and share God's good news with others.

CONTEMPORARY OPTIONS

Contemporary Gathering Words (Jeremiah 31, Psalm 119)
The word of the Lord is good for us!
It's written on our hearts!
The word of the Lord is our meditation.
Sweeter than honey is the word of God!
Come, people of God.
Come celebrate God's new covenant.
**God will write words of life upon our hearts,
and guide us all the days of our lives!**

Praise Sentences (Jeremiah 31, Psalm 119)
The word of God will teach us
and prepare us for God's good work.
**Be patient, be persistent,
and encourage all you meet.**
The heavens and the earth show the creativity of God.
**God's truth is beyond all words,
higher than the mountains
and deeper than the mighty seas.**

Praise Sentences (Jeremiah 31)
God is in our hearts!
God is in our lives!
God is in our world!
Thanks be to God!
(B. J. Beu)

OCTOBER 27, 2013

Twenty-third Sunday after Pentecost / Reformation Sunday

Hans Holznagel

COLOR

Green

SCRIPTURE READINGS

Joel 2:23-32; Psalm 65; 2 Timothy 4:6-8, 16-18; Luke 18:9-14

THEME IDEAS

Those who think boldly about Reformation Sunday might find here an invitation to re-form an ancient Judeo-Christian vocation of caring for the temple. What if the temple is God's bountiful earth? What if the earth is the temple where God's people should be satisfied, where a righteous prayer of confession is offered? What dreams, visions, and prophecies might lead humanity to repent of habits that worsen this dwelling place, reclaiming instead the bounty and goodness of God's house?

INVITATION AND GATHERING

Call to Worship (Psalm 65, Joel 2)
Praise is due to you, O God, O you who answer prayer.
Happy are those who live in your courts—
those who are satisfied with the goodness
of your house and your holy temple.

You are the hope of all things, Holy One,
from the ends of the earth to the farthest seas.
**You make the gateways of the evening
and the morning shout for joy.**
Rejoice in God, O people, and be glad.
Let us shout and sing together for joy.

Opening Prayer (Joel 2)

God of all generations,
on this Reformation Sunday,
we remember mothers and fathers in the faith
who took bold steps in new directions
to re-form your church.
Pour out your spirit upon us,
that we too may dream dreams, see visions,
and view the whole created order
as your bountiful temple.
With responsibility and joy,
we pledge ourselves to renew this temple,
in Jesus' name. Amen.

PROCLAMATION AND RESPONSE

Prayer of Confession (Psalm 65, Joel 2, Luke 18)

Creator God,
we confess this day to engaging in habits
that diminish the bounty of your creation.
Not satisfied with the goodness of your holy temple,
your seas and mountains, your rain and soil,
we have fashioned a system of sustenance
that seems good to us,
but cannot be sustained.
Be merciful to us, for we have sinned.
Answer us with awesome deeds of deliverance,
O Hope of the Earth.
Give us vision and a prophetic spirit.
Renew our vocation,
as stewards of your creation. Amen.

Words of Assurance (Luke 18, Psalm 65)
Do not lose heart.
Those who humbly admit their sins
    find favor with God.
For God answers prayer, and forgives transgression.
Believe this good news:
    We are forgiven and freed to newness of life.

Response to the Word (Psalm 65)
Enrich us with wisdom,
    and bless us with growth,
        O God of our salvation.

THANKSGIVING AND COMMUNION

Invitation to the Offering (Psalm 65)
Aware of the bounty of God's created earth, we are invited
now to give generously from our abundance. Let us share
God's blessings, as we collect our tithes and offerings.

Offering Prayer (Joel 2)
Whatever challenges we face, O God,
    we have also known your many blessings—
        threshing floors full of grain,
        vats overflowing with wine and oil.
Accept these gifts as tokens of our thankfulness,
    that they may be used to prophesy in your spirit
        and to share your bounty with those in need.
    Amen.

SENDING FORTH

Benediction (Psalm 65:12-13, Joel 2)
Breathe in the words of the psalmist:
    "The pastures of the wilderness overflow,
        the hills gird themselves with joy,
        the meadows clothe themselves with flocks,
        the valleys deck themselves with grain,
        they shout and sing together for joy."

Let these words fill you as you go forth,
   inspiring you to do no less.
Dream dreams, see visions, renew God's temple,
   God's church, God's earth.
Go in peace.

CONTEMPORARY OPTIONS

Contemporary Gathering Words (Psalm 65, Joel 2)
Here is your invitation.
Unplug in this moment from daily life:
   from display screens and overload,
   from earphones and isolation.
Reconnect to visions and dreams:
   meadows and pastures, hills and valleys,
   mountains and seas.
Reconnect to the bounty of God.
Be glad and rejoice in God.

Praise Sentences (Joel 2, Psalm 65)
Men and women, old and young,
see God's visions, dream God's dreams.
   Young and old, women and men,
   feel the Spirit fall like rain.
People everywhere on earth,
join creation, shout for joy:
   Praise is due you, O God,
   for all that you do,
   for all that you have done,
   for all that you promise to do.

NOVEMBER 1, 2013

All Saints Day
Mary J. Scifres

COLOR

White

SCRIPTURE READINGS

Daniel 7:1-3, 15-18; Psalm 149; Ephesians 1:11-23; Luke 6:20-31

THEME IDEAS

The inheritance of the saints pervades today's scriptures, yet understanding that inheritance is a challenge. For many Christians, when facing death and remembrance, we find comfort in the idea that our inheritance is a heavenly home with God. Yet, the "kingdom" we are promised is much more than a promised afterlife. Perhaps the inheritance is to praise God's glory, both now and forevermore, as Ephesians 1:12 suggests. Perhaps the inheritance is actual growth in godliness and humility, that we might be one with those whom Luke calls "blessed." If so, I pray with Paul's words to the Ephesians that God may give us all a spirit of wisdom and revelation, as we grow in our love and knowledge of Christ, and as we lead others on that journey. In this growth, we discern the hope to which we are called, the hope that called those who came before us. When we are part of this lineage of hope, surely we are both blessed and a blessing!

INVITATION AND GATHERING

Call to Worship (Psalm 149)

Come into God's presence with singing and praise.
We join the assembly of faithful followers.
Bring dancing and melody, joy and laughter.
We join the hope-filled saints of God.
Sing a new song to God, even as we remember
and proclaim ancient wisdom.
We join in the lineage of faith.

Opening Prayer (Psalm 149, Luke 6, Ephesians 1)

God of ages past and days yet to come,
    we come into your presence
        with joy and thanksgiving.
For those who have gone before us,
    we gratefully remember their wisdom.
For those who will follow after us,
    we fervently pray for their growth in faith.
For those of us here and now,
    we offer you our lives,
    that we may be faithful followers,
        true disciples, and blessed children
            of your love.
In Christ's name, we pray. Amen.

PROCLAMATION AND RESPONSE

Prayer of Confession (Ephesians 1, Luke 6)

Merciful God,
    may we never forget those who sacrificed much,
        that we might have lives of abundance
        and hope.
When we take our many blessings for granted,
    forgive us.
When we forget the many people
    who have touched and strengthened our lives
        with your love and Christ's wisdom,
            gently remind us.

Guide our steps, O God,
    that we may walk in the ways of blessedness.
Strengthen our spirits,
    that we may trust and follow your guidance.

Words of Assurance (Ephesians 1)

In Christ, we have already obtained an inheritance
    of hope and love.
Trust in the Lord. Rest in God's grace.
You are forgiven and made new in Christ!

Passing the Peace of Christ (All Saints)

Beloved saints, we are all God's children, made one in
Christ Jesus. Let us share signs of unity and love, as we
share the peace of Christ with one another.

Prayer of Preparation (Ephesians 1, Luke 6)

O Wisdom on High,
    grant us your spirit of wisdom and knowledge,
        that we may hear your word
            and bear the fruit of its power.
Open the eyes of our hearts,
    that we may discern the hope
        to which we are called.
Set free the spirit within us,
    that we may share the riches
        of your glorious, powerful love
            throughout the world.
Mark us with the seal of your Holy Spirit,
    that we may be your children,
        walking the paths of blessedness
            with the saints who have gone before. Amen.

Response to the Word (Ephesians 1, Luke 6)

Blessed are you who are poor.
    For God's kingdom is already in your midst.
Blessed are you who are hungry.
    For God's abundance is promised to you.
Blessed are you who weep.
    For joy comes with the morning.

Blessed are you who are reviled
for living the teaching of our Lord.
For you are already saints in God's kingdom.
Blessed are we when we trust in God's promises.
May we live in this glorious hope!

THANKSGIVING AND COMMUNION

Invitation to the Offering (Luke 6)

"Woe to you who are rich!" Jesus says, "for you have received your consolation." To find true consolation and joy
in our worldly riches, we must share from our abundance
with those who need it most. Come, rich or poor, for you
are welcome here. Give, rich or poor, for your gifts are
needed by God.

Offering Prayer (Luke 6)

Blessed are these gifts
    when they bring hope to the poor,
    food to the hungry,
    and comfort to the sorrowful.
May these gifts be blessed, O God,
    as they become blessings to a world in need.
In Christ's name, we pray. Amen.

Great Thanksgiving

The Lord be with you.
    And also with you.
Lift up your hearts.
    We lift them up to the Lord.
Let us give thanks to the Lord our God.
    It is right to give our thanks and praise.

It is right, and a good and joyful thing,
    always and everywhere to give thanks to you,
    God of the saints, creator of heaven and earth.
From the ancient dreams of Daniel
    to the journeys of Jesus,
    you have revealed your mighty presence to us.

When your people ignored your dreams and visions,
and when they placed their trust in earthly kings,
you came to us as a Mighty King,
revealing the truth and glory of your powerful love.
Through the law and prophets,
through saints and sinners,
you have taught us to be your people.
In love and mercy, you speak truth and blessing,
constantly renewing your covenant with us.

And so, with your people on earth,
and all the company of saints in heaven,
we praise your name
and join their unending hymn, saying:
Holy, holy, holy Lord, God of power and might,
heaven and earth are full of your glory.
Hosanna in the highest. Blessed is the one
who comes in the name of the Lord.
Hosanna in the highest.

Holy are you and blessed is your holy name.
In the fullness of time, you sent Jesus Christ
to reveal your powerful love in the world,
to show us the path of saintliness and holy living.
In humility and love, with justice and power,
Christ revealed your kingdom,
and calls us to kingdom living, even now.
Through Christ's powerful love and endless grace,
we are invited into your presence,
rescued from our sins, and led on your path
of justice and righteousness,
that we may rejoice with the saints of your kingdom.
We, who are both saint and sinner, blessed and cursed,
come to you in our joys and in our sorrows,
with thanksgiving and hope,
remembering how Jesus shared bread and wine,
even when he faced the sinfulness of his disciples.

On the night before his death, Jesus took bread,
    gave thanks to you, broke the bread,
    and gave it to the disciples—
    each of them part saint and part sinner.
Jesus said to every one of them,
    "Take, eat; this is my body which is given for you.
    Do this in remembrance of me."
When the supper was over, Jesus took the cup,
    and giving thanks to you, shared the cup
    with those same imperfect disciples.
    "Drink from this, all of you;
    this is my life in the new covenant,
    poured out for you and for many
    for the forgiveness of sins.
    Do this, as often as you drink it,
    in remembrance of me."

And so, in remembrance of these
    your mighty acts of love and grace,
    we offer ourselves in praise and thanksgiving,
    as saints and sinners in love with you,
    praying for union with Christ,
    even as we proclaim the mystery of faith.
    Christ has died.
    Christ is risen.
    Christ will come again.

COMMUNION PRAYER

Pour out your Holy Spirit
    on all of us gathered here,
        and on these gifts of bread and wine.
Make them be for us the life and love of Christ,
    that we may be for the world the body of Christ,
        redeemed, renewed, and blessed
            by your love and grace.
By your Spirit, make us one with Christ,
    one with each other,

and one in ministry to all the world,
until Christ comes in final victory
and we feast at the heavenly banquet,
with the saints of your church
and the many blessed by your grace.
Through Jesus Christ,
with the Holy Spirit in your holy Church,
all honor and glory is yours, Almighty God,
now and forever more. Amen.

Giving the Bread and Cup
(The bread and juice are given to the people, with these or other
words of blessing.)
The life of Christ, living in you.
The love of Christ, flowing through you.

SENDING FORTH

Benediction (Ephesians 1)
May we know the hope
to which Christ is calling us.
May we walk on the paths
to which God is leading us.
May we grow in the wisdom and truth
that God's Spirit is teaching us.
May we live the love
that has transformed our lives!

CONTEMPORARY OPTIONS

Contemporary Gathering Words (Luke 6)
Blessings and woes, sorrows and joys—
life has called us here.
Bless us, O God, to live in your love.
Dreams and visions, worries and fears—
life has called us here.
Bless us, O God, to live in your love.
Saints and sinners, friends and foes—
life has called us here.

Bless us, O God, to live in your love.
Giving and taking, cursing and praying—
life has called us here.
Bless us, O God, to live in your love.
Come, whoever you are, wherever you are—
God calls and welcomes you here.

Praise Sentences (Psalm 149)

Praise our God! Sing a new song of joy!
Praise our God! Sing a new song of joy!
Praise God with laughter and dance!
Praise God with laughter and dance!

NOVEMBER 3, 2013

Twenty-fourth Sunday after Pentecost
B. J. Beu

COLOR
Green

SCRIPTURE READINGS
Habakkuk 1:1-4; 2:1-4; Psalm 119:137-144; 2 Thessalonians 1:1-4, 11-12; Luke 19:1-10

THEME IDEAS
Watching and waiting is central to the spiritual life. In the face of injustice and abuse by the powerful, Habakkuk declares that he will watch and wait until God answers his petition for justice. In response to Habakkuk's vigil, God promises a vision that does not lie—a vision where the righteous shall live by faith. Zacchaeus climbs a tree as he waits to see Jesus. In response, salvation comes to his house that day. The psalmist proclaims God's righteousness and delight in God's precepts. It is a virtual certainty that the righteousness proclaimed by the psalmist came to pass while a person of faith watched and waited in prayerful expectation.

INVITATION AND GATHERING

Call to Worship (Habakkuk 1, 2)
Stand at your watchpost and wait for the Lord.
We wait for a vision of truth and hope.

Stand at your watchpost and pray to the Lord.
We pray for righteousness and understanding.
Stand at your watchpost and trust in the Lord.
We trust the One who hears our cries
and makes justice prevail.
Stand at your watchpost and wait for the Lord.

Opening Prayer (Habakkuk 1, Psalm 119, Luke 19)
God of righteousness,
    hear our prayer.
We come before you with zeal in our hearts,
    seeking justice for the wronged,
        hope for the downhearted,
            and healing for the afflicted.
We strain to see your face,
    and behold the glory of your salvation.
Visit us in our need,
    and transform us in your image,
        that salvation may come to our house this day,
            through the power of your Holy Spirit.
Amen.

PROCLAMATION AND RESPONSE

Prayer of Confession (Habakkuk 1, Luke 19)
God of new beginnings,
    come to us in our need,
        for we are weary and afraid;
    hear our pleas for mercy,
        for we are beaten down by hatred and violence;
    respond to our longing for friendship,
        for we are lonely and depressed.
God of endless love,
    visit our hearts this day,
        and shower us with forgiveness and mercy,
            that our lives may be mended
                and set on the path of salvation,
                    through the glory of your Son.

Words of Assurance *(Luke 19)*

Christ came to save the least and the lost.
Christ came to save the hopeful and the expectant—
   those who long for fullness of life.
Today, salvation has come to this house of worship,
   for in Christ, we are God's beloved children,
   forgiven and made whole,
   through the power of the Holy Spirit.

Passing the Peace *(2 Thessalonians 1:2)*

Grace to you, and peace from God, our heavenly Mother
and Father, and from our Lord Jesus Christ. In thanksgiving and praise for God's abundant blessings, share God's
grace and peace with one another.

Response to the Word or Benediction *(2 Thessalonians 1)*

With steadfast love and abundant grace,
hear God's word as people of faith.
   With prayers of hope and songs of joy,
   we will live God's word as people of promise.
With acts of grace and works of the Spirit,
share God's word as people of peace.
   Amen!

THANKSGIVING AND COMMUNION

Offering Prayer *(Psalm 119, Luke 19)*

God of many blessings,
   like Zacchaeus before us,
      we long to see your face
      and know the power of your presence.
You meet us here,
   in moments of sharing and generosity,
      to reveal a vision
      of how our lives and world might be.
Come to us and abide in our homes,
   that our lives might conform to your purposes.
Work within these offerings,
   that the world may know
      your love and justice. Amen.

SENDING FORTH

Benediction (Habakkuk 1, 2)
Though the night seems long,
watch and wait for the Lord.
Christ is coming soon!
Though hatred and violence
seem to have the upper hand.
Christ is coming soon!
Though the wicked surround the righteous,
and justice seems perverted.
Christ is coming soon!
Take heart, people of God.
Christ is coming soon!

CONTEMPORARY OPTIONS

Contemporary Gathering Words (Luke 19)
When we have to climb a tree to look for help,
Christ proclaims:
I am coming to your house today!
When we feel lost, and have nowhere to turn,
Christ assures us:
I am coming to your house today!
Christ is coming. Christ is with us even now.
Worship the Lord with joy and praise!

Praise Sentences (Habakkuk 2, Psalm 119)
With abiding love,
sing glory to our God.
With expectant faithfulness,
proclaim God's justice and righteousness.
With lasting peace,
worship the God of our salvation.

NOVEMBER 10, 2013
Twenty-fifth Sunday after Pentecost
B. J. Beu

COLOR
Green

SCRIPTURE READINGS
Haggai 1:15b–2:9; Psalm 145:1-5, 17-21; 2 Thessalonians 2:1-5, 13-17; Luke 20:27-38

THEME IDEAS
Hope for the future focuses today's readings. Facing distress at the destruction of the temple in Jerusalem, Haggai proclaims that the new temple will be made even greater than the old. Extolling God's greatness, the psalmist proclaims that God will save the faithful. The Epistle calms the fears of early Christians who are in crisis over the delay in the Lord's return. Sanctified by God's Spirit as the first fruits of salvation, we have nothing to fear. Finally, Jesus confirms the truth of the resurrection, proclaiming that our God is the God of the living, not the dead. Those who rise again are like angels who can no longer die. In the midst of anxiety and loss, hope still carries the day.

INVITATION AND GATHERING   2/1/15

Call to Worship (Haggai 1, 2 Thessalonians 2)
Though the earth shakes, and the heavens tremble,
God is always with us.

Though the seas roar and the land shudders,
God will see us through.
Though timbers splinter and temple walls crumble,
God's Spirit abides among us.
Though the world tells us we have lost everything,
God sanctifies us with the Holy Spirit.
Come, let us worship the One who never leaves us.

Opening Prayer (Haggai 1, Psalm 145)

Redeemer God,
bless us as we sing your praises
and declare the wonder of your handiwork—
for your glory fills our souls with hope,
your Spirit makes all things new.
Shake the heavens and earth once more,
that we may see your power
and lay aside our fears.
For you are greater than our fears, O God,
your majesty fills our lives with splendor.
Bring us back from death to life, Holy One,
for you are God of the living,
not the dead. Amen.

PROCLAMATION AND RESPONSE

Prayer of Confession (2 Thessalonians 2)

Living God,
our hopes are easily discouraged,
our confidence is quickly shaken,
our faith is as fragile as a tender reed.
When our footsteps falter,
remind us that we are your beloved children,
the handiwork of your gracious love.
When the odds seem stacked against us,
and we are about to lose our courage,
give us the strength to stand firm
and hold fast to your promises.
Forgive us when we cannot see in ourselves
the fruit of your salvation working within us.

Help us be the people you would have us be,
through Jesus Christ our Lord. Amen.

Words of Assurance (2 Thessalonians 2)
Hear the good news: Through the Holy Spirit,
God bears the fruit of salvation in our lives.
The One who loves us is faithful.
In Christ, our sins are forgiven. Amen.

Response to the Word (2 Thessalonians 2)
Eternal God,
your truth is as constant as the North Star,
your precepts are as solid
as the foundation of the earth.
Help us hear and follow your word
amid the voices that would deceive us.
Grow in our lives and sanctify us with your Holy Spirit,
that the fruit of your salvation may grow within us.
Amen.

THANKSGIVING AND COMMUNION

Offering Prayer (Psalm 145, 2 Thessalonians 2, Luke 20)
Caretaker of all people,
you are near to those who call you.
In a world of broken lives and unrealized dreams,
may our love reach those in need
of your hope for the future.
Use these offerings to bring justice to a world
that knows so much injustice.
Transform these gifts of money
into the fruit of salvation for those in need,
that all may know the power of your Spirit.
Amen.

SENDING FORTH

Benediction (Haggai 1)
Take courage, for God is with us.
God's Spirit moves among us.

Have faith, for God offers us abundant blessings.
God's Spirit lives within us.
Rest secure each night, for God restores our hope.
God's Spirit makes us whole.

CONTEMPORARY OPTIONS

Contemporary Gathering Words (Psalm 145)
Our God is lord and king.
We will praise God's name forever.
God's greatness knows no bounds.
We will sing of God's mighty deeds.
God protects us in watches of the night.
We will proclaim God's glory in the morning.
God saves us from our enemies.
We will shout God's majesty in the evening.
Our God is Lord and King.
We will praise God's name forever!

Praise Sentences (Psalm 145)
Great is the Lord, and greatly to be praised.
Shout praises to our Lord!
Great is the Lord, and wondrous are God's works.
Shout praises to our King!
Great is the Lord, and holy is God's name.
Shout praises to our God!

NOVEMBER 17, 2013

Twenty-sixth Sunday after Pentecost

B. J. Beu

COLOR

Green

SCRIPTURE READINGS

Isaiah 65:17-25; Isaiah 12; 2 Thessalonians 3:6-13; Luke 21:5-19

THEME IDEAS

Isaiah proclaims that God is about to create a new heaven and a new earth—the peaceable kingdom where the wolf and the lamb will feed together and everyone will have enough to eat. The psalmist urges us to shout for joy at our salvation. So far, the scriptures hang together nicely. But then Paul chastises the Christians in Thessalonica to get off their duffs and work for their bread. And Jesus proclaims that war and martyrdom are coming, along with famine and plague. Either the lectionary folks were having an off day, or they were pointing to the contradictory nature of life: New life is at hand . . . yet, death is near; God's people will be blessed with plenty and live to a ripe old age . . . yet, the faithful will die at the hands of the unrighteous in the midst of famine and plague. As Dickens said: "It was the best of times, it was the worst of times." We live our lives between the poles of hope and despair, between visions of what can be and what may be if it all goes horribly wrong. Through it all, we are called to be faithful, for we are given this promise if we endure the time of trial: "not a hair of your head will perish. By your endurance you will gain your souls" (Luke 21:18-19).

INVITATION AND GATHERING

Call to Worship (Isaiah 65, Isaiah 12)
Rejoice and be glad, people of God.
God is making all things new.
Shout aloud and sing for joy, followers of Christ.
God offers us water from the well of salvation.
Sing praises to the Lord, children of the Spirit.
God has turned our sorrow into laughter.
Rejoice and be glad, people of God.
God is making all things new.

Opening Prayer (Isaiah 65, Isaiah 12)
Eternal God,
your anger may last for a moment,
but your mercy lasts a lifetime.
With joyful hearts,
we draw living water
from the well of your salvation.
With thankful spirits,
we sing your praises
for all the world to hear.
Draw us together in this time of worship,
that we may abide in the new earth
you are creating in our midst.
Touch us with the love of your new heaven,
that we may be fit to dwell
in your peaceable kingdom. Amen.

PROCLAMATION AND RESPONSE

Prayer of Confession (Isaiah 65, Isaiah 12, Luke 21)
God of hope and promise,
speak to us again

your words of life and death,
for when we hear reports
of war, pestilence, and plague,
we become paralyzed by fear.
Bless us anew with visions of comfort and peace,
as we drink from the well of your salvation,
for we have long since had much hope
that the world will be healed
and your people will live in peace.
Even as we witness nation rise up against nation,
even as we watch earthquakes and floods
ravage the land,
open our eyes to see your new heaven
and new earth among us,
in simple acts of kindness
and gifts of tender mercy.
Make us your kingdom people, O God,
and we will be whole once more. Amen.

—OR—

Prayer of Confession (Isaiah 65, Luke 21))
O God,
we are more like the vision in Luke
than the vision of Isaiah.
We see wars, hatred, and violence everywhere,
yet despair of ever stopping them.
We see oppression and injustice and persecution,
but fail to raise our voices in prophetic protest.
We have become a pessimistic people.
Help us believe, really believe—
in Isaiah's vision of the peaceable kin-dom,
in your promise of a new heaven and new earth.
Let your cry be our cry:
"They shall not hurt or destroy
on all my holy mountain." Amen.
(Joanne Carlson Brown)

Words of Assurance (Isaiah 12:3, Luke 21:19)

With joy, we draw the waters of forgiveness and grace
   from the well of our salvation.
Christ promises that the faithful will not perish.
Indeed, through our endurance, we gain our souls.
Rejoice in the good news:
   The One we worship is faithful.

Passing the Peace of Christ (Isaiah 65:25)

"The wolf and the lamb shall feed together, the lion shall
eat straw like the ox. . . . They shall not hurt or destroy on
all my holy mountain, says the LORD." God is able to heal
all divisions and bridge all chasms that separate us. Turn
and greet one another in the spirit of reconciliation and
peace.

Response to the Word (Isaiah 65, Luke 21)

Your new heaven and new earth beckons, O God.
In the midst of war, famine, and plague,
   call us into your future with hope and expectation,
      that we may joyously work to bring your realm
         which has no end. Amen.

THANKSGIVING AND COMMUNION

Offering Prayer (Isaiah 65)

God of visions and dreams,
   your promise of a new heaven and a new earth
      feels like the unreality of sleep
         to those who have forgotten how to dream.
We long to make a difference in our world,
   but have forgotten how to see hopelessness
      as the real illusion in life—
         for in your love,
            all things are possible.
Work within our offerings this day,
   that they may be signs of our commitment
      to dream your Dreams for our world.
Work within these gifts, we pray,

that those who have lost all hope—
   even hope for a better future
      for themselves and their children—
         may find the vision and courage
            to live with passion and purpose.
Amen.

SENDING FORTH

Benediction (Isaiah 65, 2 Thessalonians 3:13, Luke 21)
Brothers and sisters in Christ,
do not grow weary in doing what is right.
   We will bring hope and love,
   justice and peace, to all we meet.
Sisters and brothers in Christ,
share God's vision of the peaceable kingdom
with a world torn by famine, war, and death.
   We will bring new vision
   to a world blinded by disappointment.
Children of God, heirs of the promise,
live this vision and dream into reality.
   We will help all who thirst
   drink from the well of salvation
   and bathe in the waters of life.

CONTEMPORARY OPTIONS

Contemporary Gathering Words (Isaiah 65, Isaiah 12, Luke 21)
Worship the One who is faithful.
   Worship God with joy.
Worship the One who fills us with every good thing.
   Worship God with song.
Worship the One who makes all things new.
   Worship God with shouts of gladness.

Praise Sentences (Isaiah 12)
Sing praises to God.
   The Holy One has done gloriously.

Sing praises to God, sing praises.
Sing God's praises in all the earth.
Shout aloud and sing for joy,
The Holy One is in our midst.
The Holy One is in our midst.
The Holy One is in our midst.

NOVEMBER 24, 2013

Reign of Christ / Christ the King Sunday

Mary J. Scifres

COLOR

White

SCRIPTURE READINGS

Jeremiah 23:1-6; Luke 1:68-79; Colossians 1:11-20; Luke 23:33-43

THEME IDEAS

Christ the King Sunday brings to mind images of royalty and power, strength and might. But our scriptures point to a different kind of ruler. Jesus offers mercy and hope to a dying criminal. Colossians reminds us that through Christ, everything on earth and in heaven has been reconciled to God. Even Jeremiah's harsh words of woe lead into the promise that a righteous Branch will guide God's people into a time of justice and righteousness. God's reign is not about the privilege of power, but justice and mercy, righteousness and love. This is the hope that Zechariah expressed as he celebrated the birth of John the Baptist and the impending birth of Jesus. This is the promise of Christ our King—the promised day when God's realm truly will come upon this earth as it is in heaven.

INVITATION AND GATHERING

Call to Worship (Luke 1, Colossians 1, Luke 23)
Dawn has broken; light has come.
Christ shines upon our lives.
The darkness is fading; new life is emerging.
Christ calls us forward in faith.
Come, let us be made strong in the strength
of Christ's glorious power.
Christ bestows the power of love,
bringing justice for all.
Truly, I tell you, we are already with God
when we live this truth.
Christ is present as we worship this day!

Opening Prayer (Jeremiah 23, Luke 1, Colossians 1)
Christ of glory and power,
we see the image of God's mercy and gentleness
in the love you shine upon our lives.
Guide us in your way of peace.
Reign in our hearts,
with your justice and righteousness.
Shepherd us as your people,
that we may display your glorious light
for all the world to see.
In the light of your powerful love, we pray. Amen.

PROCLAMATION AND RESPONSE

Prayer of Confession (Jeremiah 23, Colossians 1, Luke 23)
Jesus, remember us
as we come into this time of prayer.
Shine the light of your truth in our lives,
that we may see where we have gone astray,
and where we have driven others
from your path of justice and righteousness.
Gather us to be your people once more.
Restore us through your mercy and grace,
that we may know we are one with God
and one with you,

through the power of the Holy Spirit.
(Silent prayer or reflection may follow.)

Words of Assurance (Colossians 1, Luke 23)

Hear Christ's word to a dying criminal:
"Truly I tell you, today you will be with me
in Paradise."
These words of promise are as true for us today
as they were for the prisoner who was crucified
with Jesus.
For in Christ, God has forgiven our sins
and reconciled us to God.

Passing the Peace of Christ (Colossians 1)

In the spirit of unity and grace, may we share signs of
unity and grace with one another:
"The love and peace of God be with you."

Introduction to the Word (Luke 1)

Christ comes to shine light in the darkness and guide our
feet in the way of peace. Listen for the word of God, that
we may walk in the path of Christ's glorious light.

Response to the Word (Jeremiah 23, Colossians 1)

Be made strong with the strength of Christ's power.
**We will endure life's tests
with patience and hope.**
Reflect the image of God's glorious love.
**We will shine with the fullness
of Christ's mercy and grace.**
Be shepherds of justice and God's guiding wisdom.
**Strengthened by Christ's power,
we will be signs of God's kingdom
here on earth!**

THANKSGIVING AND COMMUNION

Offering Prayer (Luke 1, Colossians 1)

Light Giver,
we offer these gifts of light and love,

that others may see your image
reflected in the ministries of our church.
Shine through these gifts
and through our lives.
Light our way,
that we may be light in your beautiful world.

SENDING FORTH

Benediction (Luke 1)

Through God's presence, dawn has broken.
Christ's light is shining still.
Go forth as children of light.
We will shine with love for all to see.

CONTEMPORARY OPTIONS

Contemporary Gathering Words (Jeremiah 23, Luke 23)

Christ the King comes as a ruler of love and mercy,
a monarch of justice and truth.
We are showered with Christ's light and love.
Christ the King comes as the Prince of Peace,
the one who welcomes strangers
and forgives criminals.
We are showered with Christ's light and love.

Praise Sentences (Jeremiah 23, Luke 1)

Blessed be our God,
who rules with justice, mercy, and love!
Blessed be our God!
Blessed be our God,
who reigns with righteousness, care, and compassion!
Blessed be our God!

NOVEMBER 28, 2013

Thanksgiving Day

Mary J. Scifres

COLOR

Red

SCRIPTURE READINGS

Deuteronomy 26:1-11; Psalm 100; Philippians 4:4-9; John 6:25-35

THEME IDEAS

Deuteronomy speaks of the bounty of the harvest. Jesus, however, points to a greater bounty—the bounteous gift of food for the soul, the bread of life that nourishes us always. Yet, a deeper reading of Deuteronomy, and a knowledge of the Israelites' history, points to this same attitude. An attitude of gratitude arises from the Hebrew people, not only because they have a bountiful harvest, but because they have been brought out of slavery into a land flowing with the milk of God's grace, and the honey of freedom. The early pilgrims celebrated more than just surviving a horrible first winter, they celebrated the greater joy of landing in a new world, flowing with the milk of grace shown in the hospitality of the Native Americans, and the honey of freedom from religious intolerance. And so, they gave thanks. As followers of Christ, we are called to be thankful in all things and at all times, as the Letter to the Philippians reminds us. John reminds us of the gift of

Christ's constant presence, living in and through us, that we might be fed with food for the soul, and bread for the journey of faithful living. Thanksgiving Day is just one day to remember the call to be grateful.

INVITATION AND GATHERING

Call to Worship (Psalm 100)
Bring joyful noises and songs of praise.
Bring gratitude and gladness this day.
We come with words of rejoicing
and songs of celebration.
We come to give thanks for the gifts of God.

Opening Prayer (Philippians 4)
Bounteous God,
    we come into your presence with joyful hearts,
        as we reflect on the abundance of your love
            and the sustaining power of your grace.
As we celebrate and rejoice,
    we remember the things we have learned
        and gifts we have received from your hand.
Plant these lessons in our lives,
    that we may be a people of gratitude,
        abounding in love for a world
            hungry for compassion.

PROCLAMATION AND RESPONSE

Prayer of Confession (Philippians 4, John 6)
God of signs and wonders,
    forgive us when we neglect the signs
        of your sustaining presence;
    have mercy upon us when we miss the wonders
        of your amazing grace.
Shower us with the bread of your compassion,
    that we may be filled with abundant love.
Work in and through us,
    that we may be living examples

of all that is honorable and true,
all that is just and pure,
and all that is pleasing and excellent.

Words of Assurance (Philippians 4)

Celebrate the bounty of God's amazing grace.
Do not worry, but give thanks to God!
It is God's pleasure to give us the kingdom.

Passing the Peace of Christ (Philippians 4)

As children of God, let us set our minds on Christ, and
share signs of the peace that passes all understanding.

Introduction to the Word (Philippians 4)

As we listen to God's word, may we allow God's peace to
guide our hearts and minds in Christ Jesus.

Response to the Word or Call to Worship (Philippians 4, John 6)

God is near. We need not fear
God is as near to us as our very breath.
God's peace is ours. We need not worry.
God's peace is with us always.
Christ's life is given, that we might have abundant life.
Christ promises that we are never alone.
Rejoice in these promises, the promises of God.
We rejoice, give thanks, and sing!

THANKSGIVING AND COMMUNION

Invitation to the Offering (Deuteronomy 26, John 6)

As we collect gifts from God's abundance, we join in a
long line of God's people who celebrate thanksgiving with
signs of generosity and compassion. May we return the
first and the best of all that we have been given, that others may know the first and best truth of life: God is love
and Christ's grace is available to all!

Offering Prayer (Deuteronomy 26)

Holy God,
with gratitude and thanks,

we offer you the first fruits of your harvest.
We bow humbly before you,
  remembering all that you have done for us,
    and acknowledging that everything we have
      comes from you.
With thanksgiving and praise,
  we offer these gifts
    to sustain and bless the work of your church,
      and to care for the poor. Amen.
(Leigh Anne Taylor)

Prayer of Thanksgiving or Response to the Word (Deuteronomy 6)

Wanderers were our ancestors, O God.
We remember their journeys of faith.
As you heard our voices in times of sorrow,
  you lifted us up and brought us forth
    into new places of promise and hope.
With signs and wonders,
  you shared with us the grace of Christ Jesus,
    and the abundance of your constant love.
We offer now our thanks and praise,
  with gifts for others who wander still.

SENDING FORTH

Benediction

Having received grace upon grace,
and God's constant love,
go forth with songs of praise.
We will share signs and wonders,
of gratitude and generosity,
that others will see Christ living through us.

—OR—

Benediction (Philippians 4)

May the peace of God, greater than any understanding,
  be with you now and forever more.
Go in peace.

CONTEMPORARY OPTIONS

Contemporary Gathering Words or Communion Litany (Philippians 4, John 6)

Thanksgiving is more than just a day.
Thankfulness is a way of living our lives.
Christ is more than just our guide.
Christ is the bread that nourishes our lives.
The peace of God is more than a phrase.
This peace is beyond our understanding.
The bread of life is given to us.
We rejoice in God's amazing grace.

Praise Sentences (Philippians 4)

Rejoice always. Rejoice in the wonders of God!
Rejoice always. Rejoice in the wonders of God!

Praise Sentences or Benediction (Philippians 4, John 6)

Rejoice, my friends.
Rejoice in God!
Rejoice in the Bread of Life!

DECEMBER 1, 2013

First Sunday of Advent
Laura Jaquith Bartlett

COLOR
Purple

SCRIPTURE READINGS
Isaiah 2:1-5; Psalm 122; Romans 13:11-14; Matthew 24:36-44

THEME IDEAS
It is with great irony that on the very week that we begin our Advent countdown to Jesus' birth, Isaiah proclaims that we have no idea when the Prince of Peace will come. The deep longing for peace echoes as surely in our twenty-first–century world as it did in Isaiah's time. Through our liturgy, we must communicate that traditional Christmas preparations are not enough. If we truly want to receive with joy the long-awaited Prince of Peace, the one who comes at an unexpected hour, we must accept the invitation to walk expectantly in the light of the Lord, each and every day of our lives.

INVITATION AND GATHERING

Call to Worship (Isaiah 2, Psalm 122)
I was glad when they said to me,
let us go to the house of the Lord!

In days to come, the mountain of the Lord's house
shall be established as the highest of the mountains.
Come, let us go up to the mountain of the Lord!

Opening Prayer (Isaiah 2, Romans 13)

When, O God, will the day of peace come?
When will the nations stream to your holy mountain
and beat their swords into plowshares?
When will the long night of war and hatred,
give way to the dawn of love, righteousness,
and joy?
We are ready for the dawn, O God.
Shine your light into our world, mighty One of peace.
Illuminate the path,
and give us the wisdom and courage
to follow your light.
We pray in the name of the Prince of Peace. Amen.

PROCLAMATION AND RESPONSE

Prayer of Confession (Isaiah 2, Psalm 122, Romans 13, Matthew 24)

God, we are ready now.
We want peace now.
We long to receive the Prince of Peace
in our world today.
But don't delay too long, Holy One,
for soon we'll be busy with parties,
and decorating, and baking, and shopping.
Our lives are crammed so full,
we find it hard to calendar you in;
we find it hard to locate the time
to welcome the Light of the World.
We need your help, O God.
Teach us to set aside our party wardrobes,
and clothe ourselves in Jesus Christ.
Guide us into true readiness,

even though we do not know the date and time,
    when true peace will reign.
Wake us up;
    shake off the cobwebs of our complacency;
      and take us with you
        on the path up your holy mountain.
Plant your peace within us,
    so that each day, each moment,
      we may be ready for the harvest of your love. Amen.

Words of Assurance (Isaiah 2)

The light of God's love shines brightly!
The invitation is given:
    Come, walk in the light.

Passing the Peace of Christ (Psalm 122:8)

The psalmist sings, "For the sake of my relatives and friends I will say, 'Peace be within you.'" Turn now to your own relatives and friends, your sisters and brothers in Christ, gathered here in the house of the Lord, and greet them with these same words: "Peace be within you."

Response to the Word (Isaiah 2, Romans 13, Matthew 24)

We do not know the year of your coming,
but we do know how to prepare.
    We must live as peacemakers.
We do not know which day peace will reign,
but we do know how to prepare.
    We must clothe ourselves with Christ.
We do not know the hour the world can breathe again,
but we do know how to prepare.
    We must live honorably at all times.
We do not know when the Prince of Peace will come,
but we do know how to prepare.
    We must pray constantly for peace
    and walk in the light of the Lord.

THANKSGIVING AND COMMUNION

Invitation to the Offering

If this Advent is to be about more than going through the motions, then we must get ready for the Prince of Peace in new and radical ways. What can we do to signal our readiness for the coming of Christ into this very place? We can start with a total commitment of our resources and our lives to the cause of God's peace in the world. When we give our financial gifts to the ministry of this church, the benefits travel widely through the connections of our denomination, but nowhere is the impact greater than in our own hearts. I invite you to use this time of offering as an opportunity to get ready for Christ's arrival.

Offering Prayer (Isaiah 2, Psalm 122, Matthew 24)

Thank you, God.
Thank you for the wake-up call,
    reminding us to be ready.
Thank you for not giving up
    on your vision of peace.
Thank you for the opportunity
    to gather each week in your house,
        that we might encourage one another
            to stay on your path.
And thank you for the opportunity
    to give these gifts for your ministry,
        that together we might help the world
            be ready to receive the Prince of Peace,
                in whose name we pray. Amen.

SENDING FORTH

Benediction (Isaiah 2, Psalm 122, Romans 13, Matthew 24)

As you leave the house of the Lord,
    open your eyes to the signs of God's presence
    all around you.

Stay awake, and be constantly ready
    to welcome the Prince of Peace.
Put on the clothes of Jesus Christ,
    and walk with the Spirit in the path of light.
Go in peace.

CONTEMPORARY OPTIONS

Contemporary Gathering Words (Matthew 24)

(This dialogue is meant for two worship leaders, the second of whom is sitting off to the side, not paying attention—perhaps texting or reading a magazine.)
Wake up! Get ready! It's almost time!
In a minute...
No, it has to be now! You're just about out of time!
Really? How much time do I have left?
Not much!
Well, exactly how much is not much?
Okay, I don't actually know when it will be,
but that doesn't matter.
What do you mean, it doesn't matter?
I need to know when!
No, you don't need to know when
and you don't even need to know how.
You just need to get ready.
Well, okay then, let's get ready!
(Move immediately into an opening song or hymn.)

Praise Sentences (Isaiah 2 Psalm 122)

Let us go to the house of the Lord.
Give thanks to the name of the Lord.
Come, let us walk in the light of the Lord!

DECEMBER 8, 2013

Second Sunday of Advent

B. J. Beu

COLOR

Purple

SCRIPTURE READINGS

Isaiah 11:1-10; Psalm 72:1-7, 18-19; Romans 15:4-13; Matthew 3:1-12

THEME IDEAS

Isaiah promises that a righteous branch shall grow out of the shoot of Jesse—a branch bringing justice and peace to all of creation. In Advent, Christians prepare to receive this branch in the birth of Jesus. Matthew warns that the peace promised by Isaiah will be accompanied by the destruction of the wicked. Indeed, the axe is already lying at the root of the tree. In the name of the one who baptizes us with fire and the Holy Spirit, it is time to lead lives worthy of repentance. Such living promises us hope for the future.

INVITATION AND GATHERING

Call to Worship (Isaiah 11)

A shoot has come forth from the stump of Jesse.

A holy branch has grown out of his roots.

The spirit of the Lord rests upon his shoulders—

the spirit of wisdom and understanding,
the spirit of counsel and might.
Righteousness is the belt around his waist.
Faithfulness is the mantle upon his shoulders.
A shoot has come forth from the stump of Jesse.
God's promised salvation is at hand.

—OR—

Call to Worship (Matthew 3)
Prepare the way of the Lord.
God's kingdom has drawn near.
Prepare the way of the Lord.
God's salvation is at hand.
Prepare the way of the Lord.
God's Spirit is among us.
Prepare the way of the Lord.
**Blessed is the one who comes
in the name of the Lord.**

Opening Prayer (Isaiah 11, Psalm 72)
Prince of Peace,
the spirit of the Lord
rests upon your shoulders:
the spirit of wisdom and understanding,
the spirit of counsel and might,
the spirit of knowledge
and the fear of the Lord.
We behold your glory in the heavens,
for your reign endures like the sun and the moon,
throughout all generations.
Breathe your passion for justice into our hearts,
that we may defend the cause of the poor,
offer deliverance to the needy,
and crush the power of the oppressor.
May your righteousness flourish
and your peace abound,
that none shall hurt or destroy
on all your holy mountain. Amen.

PROCLAMATION AND RESPONSE

Prayer of Confession (Matthew 3)

Living God,
  we hear the words of John the Baptist:
    "Repent, for the kingdom of heaven
    has come near"—
      but we act as if these words
      were meant for others,
        not for us;
  we hear the plea of the prophet of old:
    "Prepare the way of the Lord,
    make his paths straight"—
      but we ponder these words
      as if they were merely metaphor,
        not a radical call to action.
Help us bear fruit worthy of repentance,
  that our lives may be transformed in holy fire,
    through our baptism in the Holy Spirit. Amen.

Words of Assurance (Psalm 72, Romans 15)

Trust the promises of God—
  promises of steadfast love and forgiveness.
Trust our inheritance in Christ—
  an inheritance of life everlasting,
  through the power of the Holy Spirit.
Rejoice and be glad!

Passing the Peace of Christ (Romans 15:7)

Welcome one another, just as Christ has welcomed you.
Greet one another with signs of peace, just as Christ has
welcomed you with the blessing of God's peace.

Response to the Word (Romans 15:4)

Whatever was written in former days was written for our
instruction, so that by steadfastness and by the encouragement of the saints of God, we might have hope. May
these words of prophecy, promise, and preparation encourage us to live lives of steadfast love and action.

THANKSGIVING AND COMMUNION

Invitation to Offering (Psalm 72)

God has done marvelous things for us. In loving gratitude, let us respond with wonder and delight by offering
our very selves back to God. With reverence and devotion, let us give generously of our gifts, that through our
offerings, God's promises might be fulfilled.

Offering Prayer (Isaiah 11)

Gracious God,
the gift of your Son
is like the sweet kiss of rain
on a barren land;
the shoot from the stump of Jesse
is like the bread of heaven
for those who are perishing.
In grateful response to these gifts,
we offer you our commitment to justice,
our solidarity with the poor,
and our pledge to assist the cause
of those who are in need.
May these gifts hasten the day
when none shall hurt or destroy
on all your holy mountain. Amen.

SENDING FORTH

Benediction (Psalm 72, Romans 15:5, 13)

May the God of steadfast love and encouragement
bless you to live in harmony with one another,
in accordance with the hope we find in Christ Jesus.
May the God of righteousness and peace
bless you like rain on the mown grass,
that justice may flourish and peace may abound.
May the God of hope and grace
fill you with joy, and peace in believing,
that you may abound in hope
by the power of the Holy Spirit.

CONTEMPORARY OPTIONS

Contemporary Gathering Words or Praise Sentences (Psalm 72, Romans 15)

Shout to the Lord.
   Praise God's holy name.
Sing to the Lord.
   Bless God's glorious name forever.
Praise the Lord.
   Praise the Lord.
Praise the Lord.
Let us worship.

Praise Sentences (Isaiah 11)

God is great.
   Sing glory to our God.
Christ the Lord is mighty.
   Shout praises to our King.
The Spirit is enthroned on high forever.
   Proclaim devotion to our God!

—OR—

Praise Sentences (Matthew 3)

God's Spirit is upon us!
God's Spirit washes over us!
God's Spirit is upon us!
God's Spirit washes over us!

DECEMBER 15, 2013

Third Sunday of Advent

Joanne Carlson Brown

COLOR

Purple

SCRIPTURE READINGS

Isaiah 35:1-10; Luke 1:47-55; James 5:7-10; Matthew 11:2-11

THEME IDEAS

According to James, we are supposed to wait for Jesus' arrival with patience, but this is hard as Christmas approaches. It is also hard to wait for the justice and healing promised in the other texts for today. We yearn for the time when people will be healed, when creation will be restored, and when justice and love will be the law of the land. Come quickly, Jesus, and turn our world upside down. We're waiting . . . and ready to help.

INVITATION AND GATHERING

Call to Worship (Isaiah 35, Luke 1, James 5, Matthew 11)
The time is coming.
  We're waiting.
The time is now. Do you see it?
  People are healed. Creation restored.
  The world turned upside down.
God-with-us calls us to see and to act.

**We're here to listen, to be transformed,
to live into God's Beloved Community.**
Let us join together in the presence
of the One who makes this all so.
Let us worship the God who is with us always.

Opening Prayer (Isaiah 35, Luke 1, Matthew 11)

God of justice, healing, and love,
we come this morning
in this season of waiting and longing and hope:
to listen for your voice,
to hear your call,
and to see transformation.
May this time of worship strengthen our resolve
to live lives of justice and radical love.
May this time of fellowship give us the courage
to do more than hear
about our world being turned upside down,
but to joyfully participate in that turning.
Come, O Come, Emmanuel. Amen.

PROCLAMATION AND PRAISE

Prayer of Confession (Isaiah 35, Luke 1, James 5, Matthew 11)

Liberating God,
we are not a patient people.
We want what we want,
and we want it now.
Bombarded by the cacophony of advertising
on radio, TV, the internet, and print media,
we find ourselves lured into thinking
that this is the world we want—
a world of material prosperity,
a world where status is measured
by our possessions and social status.
But that is not the world you desire.
Love, justice, healing, the restoration of creation—
this is your heart's desire.

Forgive us for being seduced by the world's messages.
Forgive us for wanting the world to stay the way it is.
Forgive us for fearing a world turned upside down.
Help us follow Jesus as we create the new reality
  of your Beloved Community,
    which is breaking into our world and our lives.
Transform us, Liberating God,
  that we may join you in transforming the world.
Amen.

Words of Assurance (Isaiah 35)
God has promised to strengthen weak hands
  and steady feeble knees.
God has called us to be strong and to put fear aside,
  for God redeems us.
God has promised us that everlasting joy will be ours,
  and sorrow and sighing will flee away.

Passing the Peace of Christ (Isaiah 35, Luke 1, Matthew 11)
Sisters and brothers, look around you. God's people are here, waiting, listening, yearning, just like you. Reach out in love and encouragement. Greet one another with joy and gladness and excitement, for God's Beloved Community is breaking forth, right here, right now in this very gathering of God's beloved people.

Prayer of Preparation
The noise of the world
  is so loud in our ears
    at this time of year.
Quiet our minds, holy One.
Open our ears and hearts
  to receive your words of love,
    re-creation, and transformation.

Response to the Word (Isaiah 35, James 5)
O God,
  for the patience to wait to see and hear;

for the words that turn our world upside down;
for the joy and gladness these words bring,
   we give you thanks and praise.

THANKSGIVING

Invitation to the Offering (Luke 1)
If Mary's words in the Magnificat are ever to come true,
we need to be part of the doing and the giving. With full
and trusting hearts, remember the promises God has
made and give gladly during this morning's offering.

Offering Prayer (Luke 1)
All that we are and all that we have
   comes from you, God of Promise and Grace.
We now return to you
   a portion of what we have been given
      to help build your Beloved Community.
But more than that,
   we offer ourselves
      as agents of your transforming love.
Use us, and use these resources,
   that our world might be turned upside down. Amen.

SENDING FORTH

Benediction (Isaiah 35, Matthew 11)
Go forth in joy and gladness and singing,
   knowing that with God as our guide and Holy Way,
   even we cannot go astray.
Go forth to tell the world
   what you have seen and heard about Jesus.
And may the Spirit strengthen you
   to join in turning the world upside down. Amen.

CONTEMPORARY OPTIONS

Contemporary Gathering Words (Isaiah 35, Luke 1)
Have you heard? It is the most amazing thing!
   What is?

The blind see. The lame walk.
Water gushes in the wilderness. Deserts bloom.
The poor are filled. The rich are sent away empty.
The powerful are thrown down.
The lowly ones are raised up.
  What can it mean?
God is turning the world upside down.
Want to join in on this?
  Absolutely!
Then come along in this time of worship.
Hear and see. Come on, let's do it!

Praise Sentences (Isaiah 35)

God is coming now to save us!
  Sing with joy and gladness!
Sorrow and sighing have fled away!
  Glory to our God forever and ever!

DECEMBER 22, 2013

Fourth Sunday of Advent

Mary J. Scifres

COLOR
Purple

SCRIPTURE READINGS
Isaiah 7:10-16; Psalm 80:1-7, 17-19; Romans 1:1-7; Matthew 1:18-25

THEME IDEAS
"Do not be afraid," the angel says to Joseph. This message of courage is the message we discover when we trust God's promises, even in the face of fear. Into the direst circumstances, God comes to be with us. Emmanuel is more than just a name for Christ or a song of praise: Emmanuel is the promise that we are not alone. We are never alone. Joseph and Mary were not alone, even as they faced the public disgrace of an unexpected premarital pregnancy, and the awesome task of raising the blessed Christ-child. God walked with them, as God walks with us. Whether people are facing a manic December or a sorrow-filled Christmas, God is present, here, now, and always.

INVITATION AND GATHERING

Call to Worship (Psalm 80, Matthew 1)
Shine forth, dear friends, for God is with us.
God is with us now!

Sing praise, sisters and brothers, for God is present.
God is with us here!
Dry your tears, children of God, for Christ has come,
and comes again.
God is with us in every time and place.

Opening Prayer (Isaiah 7, Psalm 80, Matthew 1)

Emmanuel,
   let your face shine upon us,
      that we might sense your presence,
        and rest in your love.
During this holy season,
   comfort and strengthen us in our worship,
      as we rejoice in the promise
        revealed in your birth.
In your holy name, we pray. Amen.

PROCLAMATION AND RESPONSE

Prayer of Confession (Psalm 80, Matthew 1)

Shepherding God,
   guide us back to the paths of your promise.
When we doubt, restore our trust.
When we fear, restore our courage.
When we feel alone,
   restore our awareness of your presence.
Help us be a Christmas people—
   a people who hear when the angels sing.
Help us be an Easter people—
   a people who trust the promise of new life.
Help us be an Emmanuel people—
   a people who believe in your constant presence.
In hope and trust, we pray. Amen.

Words of Assurance (Matthew 1)

Do not be afraid, dear friends.
God is with us, now and forevermore.
Christ's grace is ours, today and always.
Emmanuel. Emmanuel. God is with us now.

Passing the Peace of Christ (Matthew 1)

Shine forth as an Emmanuel people, with signs of Christ's presence in the world. Let us share signs of God's peace and love.

Introduction to the Word (Psalm 80, Matthew 1)

Give ear to God, even as God has given ear to you. Listen for God's word. Look for signs of Christ's presence. Know that God is with us now.

Response to the Word (Matthew 1)

Do not be afraid, Christ is coming soon.
Christ is with us even now.
Trust in this: The Spirit gives us a child.
Christ is born anew in our hearts.
Fear not, dear friends, for Christmas is coming.
Christmas is with us even now.

THANKSGIVING AND COMMUNION

Offering Prayer (Matthew 1)

Giver of life and love,
    receive these gifts as early Christmas gifts—
        gifts for all who will be touched and supported
            by the ministries of this church.
Bless our offerings of treasure, time, and talent,
    that we may be blessings of your presence,
        active in service to a world in need
            of your love and grace.
Be with us, we pray. Amen.

Invitation to Communion (Matthew 1)

In the breaking of the bread,
God is with us.
In the sharing of the cup,
Christ is with us.
In the unity of the body,
the Spirit is present.
Come, Emmanuel, come.

Communion Prayer or Offering Prayer (Matthew 1)

Come, Emmanuel, come.
Bless these gifts with your presence,
    that we may be an Emmanuel people:
        nourished by your grace,
        imbued with your love,
            and entrusted with your calling.

SENDING FORTH

Benediction (Matthew 1, Christmas)

Shine forth, people of God!
We shine with the presence of God.
Shine forth, followers of Christ!
We shine with Christmas joy.
Shine forth, children of the Spirit!
We shine with hope and love.
Shine forth as Emmanuel people.
Shine through us, Emmanuel. Shine!

CONTEMPORARY OPTIONS

Contemporary Gathering Words (Psalm 80, Matthew 1)

Listen for God, for God is here.
God is with us, Emmanuel.
Look for Christ, for Christ is here.
God is with us, Emmanuel.
Wait for the Spirit, for the Spirit is here.
God is with us, Emmanuel.

Praise Sentences (Matthew 1)

Emmanuel, God is with us!
Emmanuel, God is with us!

—OR—

Praise Sentences or Benediction (Psalm 80)

Shine forth with hope and love!
Shine forth with hope and love!

DECEMBER 24, 2013

Christmas Eve
Bill Hoppe

COLOR
White

SCRIPTURE READINGS
Isaiah 9:2-7; Psalm 96; Titus 2:11-14; Luke 2:1-20

THEME IDEAS
Darkness is overcome by light; despair gives way to hope; prisoners are freed; and death is vanquished by the promise of salvation. These are the life- and history-changing forces set in motion by the birth of a child—a child born to a poor Jewish couple, in an obscure town, in a backwater province of the Roman empire. On this night, we eagerly await the arrival of light, hope, freedom, and salvation, as we hear again the beloved story told and retold for generations: Christ is born! Alleluia!

INVITATION AND GATHERING

Call to Worship (Isaiah 9, Luke 2)
Good news! Unspeakable joy!
A great light has burst forth,
overcoming the darkness!
A child is born for us—a son has been given!
Bringing a kingdom of endless peace,

we shall call him Wonderful Counselor,
Mighty God!
Come, let us see what God has brought us!
Let us see what the Lord has done!
Glory to God in the highest!
And on earth, peace and goodwill to all!

Opening Prayer (Psalm 96, Isaiah 9, Titus 2)
Holy One,
you have appeared in the flesh,
bringing redemption to all,
your glory is made known in this newborn child,
this living, blessed hope.
Tonight we sing a new song—
a song of justice, righteousness, and endless peace.
Gift of God, beautiful Christ-child,
we welcome you!
Let love be born anew in our hearts
on this joyous night. Amen.

PROCLAMATION AND RESPONSE

Prayer of Confession (Isaiah 9, Titus 2, Luke 2)
Lord, we have lived far too long
in dark places of our own making.
We have walled ourselves in,
shut the world out,
and held ourselves captive
to our fear and failings.
Free us from this place, Lord.
Return us to a life in your presence,
where we may face the trials of this world
with you by our side.
Restore your light to our eyes,
that we may behold anew
your love in our lives.
Hear us and help us, we pray.
We wait in eager anticipation,
for the glory of your salvation this night. Amen.

Words of Assurance (Isaiah 9, Luke 2)
Rejoice and be glad:
  Your burdens are lifted, your captivity is ended!
The Lord's great light pierces the darkness:
  breaching the walls of our prisons,
  revealing the way of true freedom.
Light, love, and salvation have come to us this night.
Christ is born, and with Christ, we are born anew!
Amen.

Introduction to the Word (Luke 2)
Over two thousand years ago, a weary world awaited its promised savior. At the appointed time, a governor's order sent the messiah's parents from Nazareth to Bethlehem. Imagine, a decree of the Roman empire becomes the means to fulfill God's prophecies. Timeless stories, timeless truths, timeless love: our messiah has come! Christ is here!

Response to the Word (Isaiah 9, Psalm 96, Luke 2)
Your glory shines around us, Lord;
  your light banishes the darkness.
We join the angels and all the heavenly host,
  worshiping you with songs of heartfelt praise.
All creation shouts the good news of great joy:
  chains are broken, burdens are lifted,
    wounds are healed.
This is God's doing.
Let the world rejoice in the goodness of the Lord! Amen.

THANKSGIVING AND COMMUNION

Offering Prayer (Psalm 96)
Blessed Lord,
  you have given us your greatest gift—
    your very Word come to earth,
      to live with us and through us;
  you have filled us with your grace and truth—
    your holy child sent to free us from our bonds.

How can we repay such divine generosity?
Receive our thanks and praise.
As you have given to us,
  so now we share your gifts and your grace
    with a world in need.
May this offering help bring your light and love
  to those who still wander in darkness. Amen.

SENDING FORTH

Benediction (Isaiah 9, Luke 2)

A child has been born for us.
God's grace has been given to us.
From a stable in Bethlehem our savior has come.
We have seen the glory of the Lord,
revealed in the face of the Christ child.
We can hardly contain our amazement.
Tell the world. Treasure the story.
Ponder it in your heart.
We will Glorify and praise God,
for all we have heard and seen!
Rejoice! Rejoice! Christ has come!
Amen!

CONTEMPORARY OPTIONS

Contemporary Gathering Words (Psalm 96, Luke 2)

Let all people sing praises to the Lord.
Let the whole world give glory to the Lord.
Let heaven rejoice. Let the whole world rejoice.
We sing for joy. The Lord is coming.
The Lord is coming. Christ is coming.
Christ is coming. Christ is here. Hallelujah!

Praise Sentences (Isaiah 9, Psalm 96, Luke 2)

Let the heavens rejoice!
Let the earth rejoice in exaltation!
Let the seas roar and the trees shout for joy!

The Lord is coming to bring righteousness and truth.
God's light has overcome the darkness!
The light shines upon us, around us, and through us.
Sing to the Lord and bless God's name!
Salvation has come! Christ has come!

DECEMBER 29, 2013

First Sunday after Christmas

B. J. Beu

COLOR
White

SCRIPTURE READINGS
Isaiah 63:7-9; Psalm 148; Hebrews 2:10-18; Matthew 2:13-23

THEME IDEAS
The saving love of God unifies these readings. Isaiah proclaims that it was no angel that saved the people of old, but the very presence of God. The psalmist proclaims that all creation praises God: heaven and earth, young and old, birds of air and every creeping thing. How can we keep from singing God's praises? Hebrews depicts the suffering of Christ for our salvation, and Matthew recounts Herod trying to rid himself of a potential rival by slaughtering children. Salvation should be treasured and celebrated all the more for the cost it entails for the innocent.

INVITATION AND GATHERING

Call to Worship (Psalm 148)
Praise the Lord from the highest heaven!
Let the sun and the moon,
and the stars in the sky,
all sing praises to our God!

Praise the Lord from the deepest valley!
Let the mountains and the hills,
the fruit trees and tall cedars,
all worship the Lord on high!
Praise the Lord from the heart of the faithful!
Let the old and the young,
the wise and the meek,
all lift their voices and sing for joy!
Worship the Lord our God, ruler of heaven and earth!

Opening Prayer (Isaiah 63, Hebrews 2, Matthew 2)
God of holy mystery,
it was no heavenly stranger
that came to save us;
it was no divine afterthought
that freed us from captivity
to aimlessness and sin;
it was no casual gesture
that fashioned our salvation.
As we laugh and sing our praises at Christmas time,
remind us once more of what you offer us:
a love born of endless searching,
a connection born of deep longing,
a future born of selfless sacrifice.
As we praise you with our lips,
and love you with our hearts,
be with us now,
for we are your people,
and you are our God. Amen.

PROCLAMATION AND RESPONSE

Prayer of Confession (Matthew 2)
Merciful God,
we rejoice with the angels
who proclaimed Christ's birth
and saved his life from Herod's soldiers,
but we pay little heed
to the death of innocent children

who are powerless to stop
the wrath of tyrants;
we celebrate the star in the heavens
that guided the wise men from the East
to the Christ child,
but we ignore the light you put within us
that can guide us to find our way
when all other lights have gone out.
Open our hearts to the plight of the innocent,
and remove the scales from our eyes
to see the needs of your children,
that we might be new creations,
transformed and reborn
in the love and joy of Christmas.

Assurance of Pardon (Isaiah 63, Psalm 148)
God is faithful and abounding in steadfast love.
In Christ, God has come to us to be our salvation.
The birth of Jesus offers us hope:
The promise of new life and pardon in his name.

Passing the Peace
Jesus claims us as brothers and sisters before the living God. Let us, in turn, claim each other as brothers and sisters in Christ, as we share signs of peace.

Introduction to the Word (Isaiah 63:7)
Let us recount the gracious deeds of God, the praiseworthy acts of the Lord, for everything the Holy One has done for us according to God's steadfast mercy.

Response to the Word (Hebrews 2)
Praise the Lord!
Praise the Lord from the highest heaven.
Praise the Lord you heavenly hosts.
Let the sun and the moon,
and all the shining stars, praise God.
Praise the Lord, O people of God.
Let all people praise the author of salvation.

THANKSGIVING AND COMMUNION

Offering Prayer (Isaiah 63, Psalm 65)
Glorious God,
> source of all that was and is and that will be,
>> we thank you for your many blessings.
You sing the stars into being
> and stretch out your hand
>> to call forth waters to cover the deep.
You plant fruit trees to feed your creatures,
> and cause the sun and moon
>> to provide warmth and light.
Your steadfast love provides everything we need
> to walk in blessedness upon the earth.
In thankfulness and praise for your many gifts,
> we offer you our love, our service,
>> and our offerings.
In the name of Christ,
> who came to be our salvation,
>> all praise and glory be unto you. Amen.

SENDING FORTH

Benediction (Isaiah 63, Matthew 2)
> As we journey through the Christmas story,
>> **more than a star guides us,**
> more than a messenger shows us the way,
>> **more than an angel shields us from harm.**
> As we live the Christmas story,
>> **more than a fairy tale touches our heart,**
> more than Santa Claus leaves gifts under the tree.
>> **When we live the truth of Christmas,**
> we touch the presence of the living God,
>> **we taste the joy of our salvation.**

CONTEMPORARY OPTIONS

Contemporary Gathering Words (Psalm 148)
> Praise God from the highest heaven.
>> **Praise God from the deepest seas.**

Praise God in the wind and the rain.
Praise God in the snow and the frost.
Praise God from the love in our heart.
Praise God from the joy in our soul.
Praise God from the sanctuary.
Praise God from the schoolyard and factory.
Let all creation praise God.
Praise God!

Praise Sentences (Christmas)

Christ is born.
Shout alleluia!
Christ is born.
Sing God's praises!
Christ is born.
Laugh with holy joy!

CONTRIBUTORS

Peter Bankson is a member of the Celebration Circle (worship) Mission Group and the Servant Leadership (staff) Team of Seekers Church in Washington, DC.

Laura Jaquith Bartlett, an ordained minister of music and worship, lives at a United Methodist retreat center in the foothills of Oregon's Mt. Hood, where she serves as the program director.

Joanne Carlson Brown is the clergy-type for Tibbetts United Methodist Church in Seattle, WA. She is also an adjunct professor at Seattle University School of Theology and Ministry and lives in Seattle with Thistle, the wee Westie.

Mary Petrina Boyd enjoys the opportunities for urban ministry as pastor of University Temple United Methodist Church in Seattle, WA. She loves to weave, spin, and sew, and works on an archaeological dig in Jordan.

Ken Burton is a member of the Celebration Circle Mission Group of Seekers Church in Washington, DC.

Kate Cudlipp is a member of the Servant Leadership Team (staff team) and the group that writes worship liturgies for Seekers Church in Washington, DC.

Robin D. Dillon received her Master of Divinity from The Methodist Theological School in Ohio and is a pastor in the East Ohio Conference of The United Methodist Church.

Karin Ellis is a United Methodist pastor who lives in Tustin, CA, with her husband and two children.

Rebecca Gaudino teaches theology at the University of Portland.

Jamie Greening is the Senior Pastor of First Baptist Church, Port Orchard, Washington, where he makes his home with his wife and two daughters.

Hans Holznagel has served in communication, mission interpretation, administrative, and fundraising roles in the national ministries of the United Church of Christ since 1984. He and his family live in Cleveland, Ohio, where they are members of Archwood United Church of Christ.

Bill Hoppe is the music coordinator for Bear Creek United Methodist Church in Woodinville, Washington, and is a member of the band BrokenWorks, for which he is the keyboardist. He thanks his family and friends for their continued love, support, and inspiration.

Amy B. Hunter is a poet, an educator, and an Episcopal layperson who is taking sabbatical time from parish work in order to write about living the Resurrection, even in suburbia.

Sara Dunning Lambert is mom, wife, nurse, child of God, and Worship Coordinator at Bear Creek United Methodist Church in Woodinville, Washington.

Sandra Miller is a worship leader at Seekers Church, a progressive Christian church in the tradition of Church of the Savior in Washington, DC. Sandra is also a member of the governing body of the church and a member of a peace and justice mission group called Eyes to See, Ears to Hear. She is also the Administrative Coordinator at Community Vision.

Matthew J. Packer is a church musician serving Flushing United Methodist Church in Flushing, Michigan, and works for the Flint District UMC as a Small Membership Church consultant. He maintains an active concert ministry through Matt Packer Live (www.mattpackerlive.com).

J. Wayne Pratt is a retired local pastor living in North Carolina. A graduate of Drew Theological School, Wayne enjoys writing liturgy, preaching, reading, and gardening.

Deborah Sokolove is the Director of the Henry Luce III Center for the Arts and Religion at Wesley Theological Seminary, where she serves as Assistant Professor of Art and Worship.

Mark Sorensen is the Director of Contemporary Worship and College and Young Adult ministries at First United Methodist Church in Shreveport, LA.

Terri Stewart is a student at Seattle University, pursuing her MDiv and a certificate in Spiritual Direction. She currently resides in Woodinville, WA, where she enjoys creative writing on matters of spirituality. You can find her at www.cloakedmonk.wordpress.com.

Leigh Anne Taylor is the Minister of Music at Blacksburg UMC and lives with her family in the mountains of southwest Virginia.

SCRIPTURE INDEX

Page numbers in italics refer to materials found online.

SCRIPTURE INDEX

COMMUNION LITURGIES INDEX

In order of appearance

SONG AND HYMN INDEX